BEGINNER'S PHOTOGRAPHY SIMPLIFIED

A MODERN PHOTOGUIDE

BEGINNER'S PHOTOGRAPHY SIMPLIFIED

by

Stuart Nordheimer

PRENTICE-HALL
Englewood Cliffs, New Jersey 07632

AMPHOTO
Garden City, New York 11530

CONTENTS

Prentice-Hall - 12/77 - 5.48

to
Helen,
the girl at the window.

FOREWORD

One day, after several months of suffering, my Instamatic camera died an ignominious death. I helped alleviate the grief by deciding to replace it with "something better," and thus got started in photography. Unfortunately, there was very little good literature published for the inept beginner. Hence, the scope of this book is to help the beginning photographer. It's language is simple and straightforward with a minimum of mind-boggling, technical details. In this way, I hope to encourage the novice photographer to stay with his hobby.

In all probability, you will decide to buy a 35mm camera. For this reason, the format of this book is biased toward 35mm photography. However, the basic information presented here is valid for other size cameras and can be used practically without modification.

Although photography is an expensive hobby, with a little bit of imagination and ingenuity, you can reduce costs significantly. There are many useful, money-saving suggestions in this book. Some may spark ideas of your own on further ways to economize.

1

CHOOSING A CAMERA

Under the assumption that you have not yet bought a camera, this chapter will deal with making your choice.

The most popular cameras sold today (other than the Polaroid and Instamatic types) are those using 35mm film. This format produces negatives or slides that are 24 x 36mm, or about 1" x 1½", and must be enlarged (blown-up) or projected for satisfactory viewing.

There are two basic designs of 35mm cameras—rangefinder and single-lens reflex—differing primarily in the manner of viewing the picture subject. Both are capable of making excellent photos.

SINGLE-LENS REFLEX CAMERAS

The single-lens reflex design is currently enjoying the strongest sales. It's greatest advantage over the rangefinder is that what you see through the viewfinder is, for all practical purposes, exactly what the film records. The single-lens reflex (SLR) uses a built-in mirror and prism that permit you to look through the lens. It is most advantageous when using telephoto lenses (see Chap. 5). This very advantage, though, is also the greatest weakness of the SLR. The mirror must move out of the light path, between the lens and film, before the shutter opens. The rapid acceleration and deceleration of the mirror causes vibrations that can degrade picture quality. The added moving parts necessary for SLR design increase the likelihood of repair or adjustment; but the reliability of modern SLR's has made this last point nearly insignificant.

RANGEFINDER CAMERAS

The rangefinder offers superior performance with wide-angle lenses in that more precise focusing is normally possible than with an SLR (see Chap. 5). A rangefinder is usually smaller and lighter than an SLR—an advantage when one is under physical stress, such as climbing a mountain. It is also reputed to be faster to use than the SLR. The major disadvantage of a rangefinder is that it can only match the SLR's "through-the-lens" viewing accuracy by the addition of costly accessories.

CAMERA ACCESSORIES

A second factor affecting your choice of cameras is the availability of accessories to fit a particular model.

Interchangeable Lenses and Mounts

For an overwhelmingly large number of photographers, a camera must have interchangeability of lenses. In all probability, you will eventually want the flexibility of various lenses. Therefore, I urge you to buy a camera that features lens interchangeability. Unfortunately, only the most expensive rangefinders, such as Leica, Canon, and Robot feature lens interchangeability.

Interchangeable lenses fasten to the bodies of cameras by a breech-lock mount, bayonet mount, or threaded mount. The bayonet and breech-lock lens mounts attach to a camera instantaneously—a definite plus. Bayonet and breech-lock mounts vary from camera to camera, thus limiting your choice of lenses. (There are some adapters available that will allow you to use more lenses on your camera.) Though the threaded lens mount takes longer to attach to a camera body, it has its virtues. First, a vast number of lenses are available to fit the "Pentax/Praktica" thread. SLR's made by Pentax, Praktica, GAF, Edixa, Mamiya/Sekor, Fujica, Olympus, Yashica, Argus, Icarex, Ricoh, and Zenit all use this particular mount. The second advantage of threaded mounts is that their precision fit allows superior results with extreme close-up photography.

Miscellaneous

Other accessories range from filters and lens shades (available for virtually all 35mm cameras) to motor drives and interchangeable viewfinders. These latter, more esoteric devices, are only available for the expensive, top lines of such cameras as Leica, Nikon, Canon, Pentax, Miranda, Olympus, and Topcon. The importance of the versatility of numerous accessories will depend upon what type of photographic work you intend to do. In most cases, though, a camera with a vast "system" of accessories will not be needed. If you think that you might want to get a systems camera someday, you could buy a simpler model camera in the manufacturer's line. This way the extra lenses and accessories that you buy now will fit the camera you buy later. For example, buy a Nikkormat now and a Nikon F2 later; or buy a Canon FTb now and a Canon F-1 later.

EXPOSURE METERS

A good picture is properly exposed; and the exposure is usually determined with an exposure meter (see Chap. 2). Nearly every 35mm camera sold today has a built-in or add-on exposure meter. Cameras usually come with "averaging," "spot-reading," "center-weighted" (sort of a semispot), or "spot and average" meters. All types are capable of supplying the exposure information you will need, but their use must be tempered with judgment. Today's trend is toward "center-weighted" meters, but no single type is truly superior. It is important to determine which meter is best for you. Chapter 2 will help you decide.

AUTOMATIC EXPOSURE CAMERAS

There are some cameras on the market that have a fully automatic exposure operation. These cameras make it possible for you to take pictures very quickly with little fumbling over camera controls. Some automatic cameras require you to choose a shutter speed (the length of time that the shutter remains open). The camera will then set the proper f/stop, or aperture (size of the lens opening through which the light passes on its way to the film). Others require you to select the f/stop. In this case, the camera will select the shutter speed electronically. Cameras that automatically select f/stops have one advantage over cameras that automatically select shutter speed—if its batteries wear out, the former camera type may still be operated manually without automatic exposure or the use of its built-in meter. When the batteries of a camera with an electronic shutter go dead, the camera cannot be operated until new batteries are installed. A disadvantage of the first type of automatic-exposure camera is that most models have shutter-release buttons that require a relatively great deal of force to push down. This force can cause camera movement that could result in blurred pictures. Fortunately, Konica's latest models have overcome this problem.

However, there are two precautions. (1) You will encounter situations, such as a backlit subject, when automatic cameras will decide upon the wrong f/stop. Therefore, if you consider buying a fully automatic camera, make sure that it has a manual override. (2) Be wary of camera store salesmen and advertisements. Some salesmen and ads, whether through ignorance or dishonesty, try to pass off conventional cameras as automatic exposure models. This error will seem credible upon inspection of the lens. In most cases, the word "automatic" or "auto" will be engraved on the lens barrel. This does not mean that the camera features automatic exposure. What it does mean will be discussed in Chapter 5 under the heading of "automatic and preset lenses." To be sure that the camera is truly automatic, consult its instruction booklet.

SHUTTERS

There are two types of shutters used in 35mm cameras—leaf and focal plane. The leaf shutter can operate at any of its speeds with electronic flash units, whereas the focal-plane shutter can do so only at its lower speeds. The leaf shutter is also quieter than the focal-plane shutter. Unfortunately, leaf shutters are normally mounted within or directly behind the lens, making the lenses for such cameras much more expensive and far less common than lenses for cameras equipped with focal-plane shutters. Consequently, most 35mm cameras have focal-plane shutters, although the leaf shutter is common on other types of camera.

STARTING OFF RIGHT

Now that you are armed with information, you can visit a camera store without fear of confusing an SLR with the CIA. But first, a few suggestions. If you live near a big city, shop prices at the many camera stores located there. You will find that tremendous discounts are available. If you find a store you like, you will discover that in exchange for your regular patronage, you can glean a wealth of free advice. Whatever you do, though, deal only with reputable stores. A reputable dealer may even have a good, used camera just right for you, thus saving you more money. But be sure that the previously owned equipment is sold with a guarantee.

One final, super-important tip on your camera purchase—*don't* be awestruck by certain brand names. The ideal camera for your uses may be much less expensive than the camera you may think you want. All that you might get for your extra money is pride of ownership and not better pictures. I still keep some photos in my portfolio that were taken with very low-cost cameras.

2

EXPOSURE

The title of this chapter does not refer to the actions of exhibitionists occasionally encountered in the subway stations of New York City. Instead, it refers to the amount of light that strikes photographic film.

Exposure is dependent upon two factors: (1) the length of time that light "shines" on film; and (2) the intensity of the light that reaches the film. These two factors are controlled by your camera's shutter speed and diaphragm opening (aperture, or *f*/stop), respectively.

For best understanding, do not proceed without your camera in front of you.

Figure 2-1

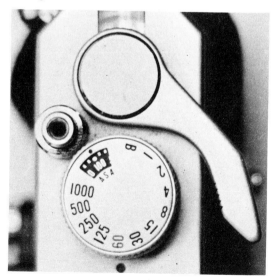

SHUTTER SPEEDS

The shutter speeds marked on your camera's shutter-speed dial vary by a factor of two (refer to Figure 2-1). That is, the next slower speed than the one selected is twice as long as the one selected, thus doubling the exposure. Conversely, the next faster speed than the one selected halves the exposure, since it is half as long as the original shutter speed. A great many cameras are capable of the following shutter speeds: B (for the old-fashioned squeeze bulb, or time exposure), 1, 1/2, 1/4, 1/8, 1/15, 1/30, 1/60, 1/125, 1/500, and 1/1000 sec. Referring to Figure 2-1, you can see that the shutter speeds engraved on the camera's control knob are not expressed as fractions of a second. Cameras don't have sufficient room to be marked in such a manner. Therefore, you should think of these numbers as denominators of fractions, all with a numerator of 1 (e.g., 500=1/500 sec., or 60=1/60 sec.).

Although not all of the speeds vary precisely by a factor of two from their adjacent speeds, they are close enough that the differences are negligible. We'll see the importance of all this information later in the chapter.

f/STOPS

The *f*/stops marked on the aperture-control ring of your lens are similar to shutter speeds in that most of these vary exposure by a factor of two. Thus, *f*/2.8 allows twice as much light through the lens than its next smallest adjacent value of *f*/4, and half as much light as *f*/2. Typical *f*/stops marked on a lens may be 2, 2.8, 4, 5.6, 8, 11, 16, 22. These are all denominators of fractions of the focal length. Hence, the smaller numbers represent larger apertures, and consequently, more exposure to light.

CONTROLLING EXPOSURE

You may wonder why camera manufacturers provide you with two ways to control exposure when either the shutter speed or the f/stop can change exposure. Herein lies a goodly portion of your being able to create something more than an ordinary snapshot.

The shutter speed that you select will capture anything from a soft blur to the razor-sharp freezing of extreme movement. The following chart will help you determine what minimum shutter speed is necessary to "stop" motion on the film. These suggested speeds are to be used as guides. You must experiment in order to expand your picture-taking capabilities.

This chart refers to subjects about 30 feet from the camera.

	movement toward or away from camera	movement diagonal to camera	movement in plane to left-right to camera
stationary to slight movement	any	any	1/30 minimum, hand-held
pedestrians and heavy traffic	1/30	1/60	1/125
runners, slow vehicles, ballet	1/125	1/250	1/500
athletic events	1/250	1/500	1/1000
fast vehicles and athletics	1/500	1/1000	see text below

STOPPING ACTION

Though it is startling, and most interesting in an academic sense, to see sharp photos that completely stop rapid motion, these photos seldom convey the feeling of speed and/or motion. Therefore, a certain amount of blurring is often both allowable and desirable. One way to accomplish this is to select a shutter speed one or two positions slower than necessary to completely stop the motion. Another way of adding the feeling of speed is to "pan" a fast-moving object (Figure 2-2). In this situation, you would first select a moderate shutter speed (perhaps 1/60 sec.). Then, smoothly moving the camera to keep the subject centered in the viewfinder, continue following the subject until it goes well beyond you. However, just before the subject is directly in front of you, trip the shutter, and continue "following" the action. It will take some

practice to do this perfectly, but the resulting photo will show a nearly stopped subject and a streaked background, clearly indicating speed. Remember to focus beforehand on the area that your subject will pass through, and be sure that you are using good exposure.

"Panning" the subject is one way that you can sufficiently stop action that is moving too fast for the shortest (highest) shutter speed of your camera. An alternate method is to snap the shutter at the "peak of action." For example, trip the shutter when a person on a swing just reaches the end of the forward movement and has not yet begun to swing back (Figure 2-3); or the brief moment when a pole vaulter is just clearing the crossbar and hasn't yet begun to fall. By observing different kinds of action, you will discover many other instances when there are relatively slow peaks of action.

Figure 2-2

16

Figure 2-3

DEPTH OF FIELD

The f/stop that you choose will affect the final picture in a completely different way than will the shutter speed. The selected aperture varies the depth of the area within a picture that appears to be in focus. This is called "depth of field." The larger the aperture (numerically small f/stop), the shallower the depth of field. The smaller the aperture (numerically large f/stop), the greater the depth of field. This is best illustrated by Figures 2-4 and 2-5. Remember that only the object you have focused on will be in focus; the rest of the detail within the depth of field will only appear to be in focus. With an SLR, you can preview the depth of field for a given aperture by setting the f/stop and switching your lens from automatic to manual mode. Be sure to focus first, though, with the lens diaphragm all the way open—the additional light coming through the lens makes focusing easier.

Most lenses are marked with a depth-of-field scale (Figures 2-6 through 2-9). The scale at the top of each picture is the distance scale. At the bottom of each picture is the aperture scale. Between them are a group of numbers and lines that are intended to help you estimate depth of field. The numbers represent f/stops.

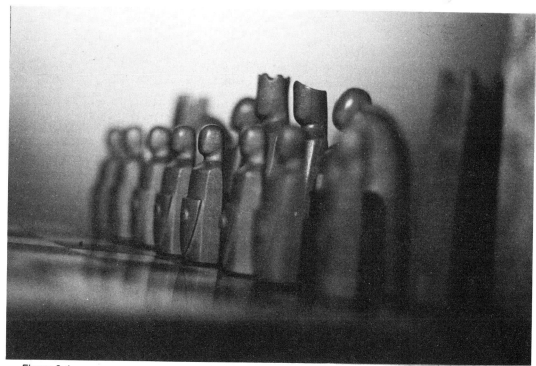

Figure 2-4

Figure 2-5

18

Figure 2-6

Figure 2-7

Figure 2-8

Figure 2-9

To estimate depth of field, focus your camera and adjust its controls for proper exposure (more on proper exposure in a moment). Then, noting what *f*/stop you have selected, find the two corresponding *f*/numbers on the middle scale. The lines leading from this scale enclose a certain area on the distance scale. The enclosed area tells you what distance range will appear in focus. For example, in Figure 2-6, the selected *f*/stop is *f*/4. The enclosed distance for *f*/4 is 12 to 9 feet. Therefore, the depth of field at this aperture and distance would be 12 to 9 feet. The depth of field for

Figures 2-7 through 2-9 would be 18 to 6³/₄ feet, 4¹/₄ feet to 3³/₄ feet, and 4³/₄ to 3¹/₂ feet, respectively.

As you can see, depth of field expands both as the aperture closes and the distance increases.

Using a large aperture, you will be able to isolate your subject, i.e., only the subject will be in sharp focus (Figure 2-10). With a small aperture, a great deal more will appear to be in focus (Figure 2-11). We'll see in the next chapter how depth of field can help you compose better photos.

Figure 2-10

Figure 2-11

PROPER EXPOSURE

The way for you to determine proper exposure is by using the exposure meter built into your camera or by using a separate hand-held meter. If you have neither one, the information sheet that is packaged with your film will provide you with some exposure guidelines.

Using your camera's meter, the first thing you should do is set the film speed on the film-speed dial. (Get into the habit of setting this dial anytime that you load film into your camera.) The film will have two equivalent laboratory-tested speed ratings: DIN, the German standard; and ASA, the American standard. These values are printed both on the film box and cartridge (Figure 2-12). Once the rating is set, the meter is properly oriented for the particular film you are using.

Next, focus on your subject. Then select either a particular shutter speed (if a certain amount of action stopping is desired). If your camera's meter has an on-off switch, turn it on. If you preselected the shutter speed, adjust the f/stop control until your meter indicates proper exposure. (Check the instructions that came with your camera to see what indication is "proper expo-

sure" with your camera. In fact, if you haven't read through the instruction manual, be sure to do so before using the camera.) If you cannot obtain a proper exposure indication, you will have to readjust both the shutter speed and the f/stop. Similarly, if you preselected an f/stop, then you will have to adjust the shutter speed until your meter indicates proper exposure. Again, if you cannot obtain a proper exposure indication, you will have to readjust both the f/stop and the shutter speed.

BUILT-IN METERS

Meters that are built into cameras are called averaging, spot, or center-weighted meters. The averaging meter measures all the light that would fill an entire frame of film and then arrives at an "average" value for the light. The spot meter measures just a small percentage of the light that will eventually fall on the film. This area is often defined by a small circle in the center of the viewfinder. A spot meter can be more useful than an averaging meter, because it can measure a selected area of a scene without having the reading affected by surrounding brightness or shadows. This feature is especially useful when trying for the proper exposure of a backlighted subject (see Chap. 4). A center-weighted meter falls somewhere between averaging and spot meters. Like an averaging meter, a center-weighted variety measures the light that would fill an entire frame of film, but it is programmed to be more sensitive to the light reflected from the middle of the picture area—hence its name.

No matter which type of meter your camera has, you will have to temper its readings with judgment. Therefore, unless a particular type of meter is important to you, don't base your choice of camera on it. Incidentally, Mamiya/Sekor DTL series, Topcon, and Miranda Sensorex EE are all equipped to measure both average and spot readings.

Figure 2-12

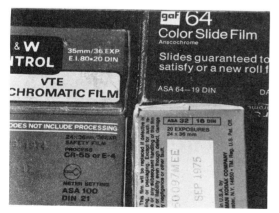

HAND-HELD METERS

Using a hand-held exposure meter, one must first set the film speed. If the meter has an on-off switch, turn on the meter. Next, point the meter's light-reading cell at the subject. Then, adjust the meter's dial according to its instructions. The resulting reading will be a series of f/stop and shutter-speed combinations, all yielding the same exposure. These combinations are often referred to as exposure value or EV. For example, f/5.6 at 1/60 sec. is equivalent to f/4 at 1/125 sec. is equivalent to f/2.8 at 1/250 sec. (Figure 2-13). As you can see in this illustration, when the shutter speed becomes shorter in duration, the aperture increases in size, and vice versa. Since a one-step adjustment of either control will vary exposure by a factor of two (remember?), you can produce photos with nearly any desired amount of depth of field or stop action. Two precautions before continuing. (1) Do not use a shutter speed slower than 1/30 sec. without some sort of solid support for the camera. The ideal support is a tripod. However, a fence, car top, or boulder will do quite nicely. When using a slower speed without support, it is likely that normal body shake will blur the picture. If there is absolutely nothing available for supporting your camera, you can control vibrations somewhat by using the "shooting" position pictured (Figure 2-14). (2) When an extremely deep or shallow depth of field is not needed for a photo, use the f/stops toward the middle of the aperture-control range. Most lenses have their best resolving power and contrast at these settings.

GRAY CARDS

All light meters are designed to give a reading that corresponds to the proper exposure for a medium gray. Therefore, if you should "meter" a blonde wearing light colored clothing in a bright snow scene, the meter will assume all the brightness is a very well-lit, medium gray scene. The meter, adjusted for medium gray, will indicate much too little exposure, and the blonde's face will be too dark to recognize. Therefore, you should make an allowance for it (introduce "guesstimation") and open up the aperture one or two stops. Or better yet, you should meter an 18% gray card. Kodak sells these cards reasonably and has manufactured them to reflect the medium gray light for which meters are adjusted. To use the card, place it in the part of the scene where proper exposure is most important (perhaps the blonde's face) and aim it toward the camera. Take a light reading from the card, being careful not to cast a shadow on the metered area, and use that reading for a properly exposed photo.

Another instance in which gray-card reading is essential is when the subject is lit from behind, or "backlighted." A "straight" metering will produce silhouettes on a bright background—great, if that was your intention. But to properly expose detail in a backlighted subject, take a reading from your gray card while it is in the subject's position, facing the camera.

Figure 2-13

LIGHT METERS

Remember that light meters are designed for average toned and lighted scenes. When you try to photograph under other than average conditions, you will have to use a gray card or "guesstimation" (a technique that you will acquire only with a lot of experience).

Most meters built into cameras and the hand-held meters described above measure light reflected from your subject and are therefore called "reflected-light" meters. "Incident-light" meters measure the light that will fall on the subject, and are aimed at the camera from the subject's position. This latter type of meter cannot be fooled, as can a reflected-light meter, and does not require the use of a gray card.

By now you should have a camera and basically know how to make it work. In the next two chapters, we will see how to make good, interesting photographs.

Figure 2-14

3

COMPOSITION

Now that you have chosen your camera and have seen how to achieve proper exposure, it is time that you learn to make good photographs instead of ordinary snapshots. This end can be reached by applying the following techniques of composition: (1) the "rule of thirds"; (2) subject posture or pose; (3) camera angle; (4) background; (5) framing; (6) selective focus; and (7) shape themes.

RULE OF THIRDS

When taking snapshots, the average camera user is very careful to center the most important part of the picture within the viewfinder. While this does guarantee that the subject will be in the picture, it does not guarantee that the photo will be interesting. In fact, it just about guarantees that the picture will be dull and boring. Instead of centering the subject in the viewfinder, one should make a point of off-centering the subject (Figures 3-1 and 3-2). This is where the rule of thirds comes in. The rule of thirds, or how best to off-center the subject, is easily understood if we look at Figure 3-3. It has been drawn with dimensions of the same ratio as a frame of 35mm film (1:1.5), with lines separating the paper horizontally and vertically in thirds. Figure 3-3 represents the viewfinder of a camera. Place the horizon along one of the horizontal lines, or place the subject at any of the four locations where the lines intersect (points A, B, C, or D), and you will have better photos.

Figure 3-1

Figure 3-2

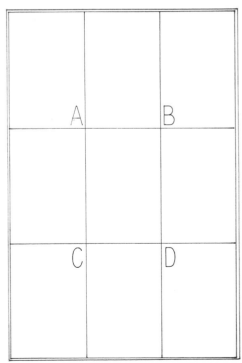

Figure 3-3

SUBJECT POSTURE OR POSE

Most people, children especially, will act strangely in the presence of a camera. Some will run away; some will turn into protoplasmic statues; some will peer back at you through the lens, standing only one or two inches away; and some will just sit and grin. To cure these problems, you should get the subjects used to having the camera around. Waste some film, or shoot without film, so that the camera will lose its novelty to the subjects. After a while they will no longer be intrigued by you and your camera. Then, you will be able to photograph them in their normal postures and expressions, capturing a truer image of them. This, of course, is not the way to "shoot" formal portraits. Please don't even try formal portraiture until you've learned a bit more. Posed photos, unless handled most skillfully, look like posed pictures—stilted and unnatural. Therefore, start off by shooting kids and people during normal activity until you can recognize unposed poses.

All right, if you feel you must shoot some formal portraits, try following these two suggestions. (1) Be sure to observe the rule of thirds, but modified as follows. In most cases, a portrait will be most appealing if you locate the subject in the viewfinder so that there is empty space in front of the subject (Figure 3-4). (2) Don't shoot portraits until you read and understand the remainder of this chapter and Chapter 4: Lighting.

Figure 3-4

Figure 3-5

Figure 3-6

CAMERA ANGLE

Another common problem encountered when taking pictures of people, or most other subjects for that matter, is the camera angle. Most poor photos of kids, when taken from the normal eye level of the photographer, look like pictures of midgets (Figure 3-5). Looking down at children from your eye level will often produce this type of distortion on film. To avoid this, get down on their level (Figure 3-6). Put on some old clothes so that you can cast off all fears of grass staining that new Brooks Brothers suit. All of a sudden, the kids will begin to look like young humans.

Figure 3-7

Figure 3-8

Figure 3-9

BACKGROUND

Another source of awful pictures is the background. Don't become so taken with your subject that you forget about the background. The background should be included in your photos so that it supplements the mood of a photo without overpowering it. A busy background will distract from your subject. Be wary of having the background appear connected to the subject. Many people may believe, upon seeing a photo, that your wife really does have a telephone pole sprouting from her head. By simply shifting your position (and the camera's), you can avoid mistakes of this sort.

There are two more things that you can do to avoid background problems. First, you can change the camera angle. If you shoot from a very low position, up at the subject, the background can be a fairly nondistracting sky (Figure 3-7). Second, you can choose a high camera angle, shooting down at your subject (be careful about creating more "young midgets"), making the ground, grass, ivy, or what have you into a simple background (Figure 3-8). For indoor pictures, you may choose either a low camera angle, causing the upper wall to become the background, or a more direct camera angle, positioning your subject in front of plain drapes or an unadorned wall (Figure 3-9).

A third method of producing an acceptable background is to create a shallow depth of field. If you choose a large aperture, anything significantly separated from the subject will be out of focus. Usually, this will produce a soft-focus, random pattern for a background (Figure 3-10).

Figure 3-10

FRAMING

The next most common subject that is improperly photographed is scenery (landscapes, seascapes, snowscapes). Unfortunately, most people's scenic shots end up looking like giant backgrounds. Upon seeing the majesty of the Grand Canyon, the average person usually steps back a ways so that he or she can get as much of the view into the picture as possible. But all that that produces is a snapshot with a very long, small canyon, viewable only through a magnifying glass. Instead of stepping back, you should move in closer to increase the area on the film that has recognizable canyon on it. You should also "frame" the subject with some object in the foreground: part of a tree filling one side and the top edge of the picture (Figure 3-11); a wild flower leaning into the scene from one side; or a group of leaves that are almost touching the lens, thereby suggesting that they are present (Figure 3-12). Again, don't forget the rule of thirds—keep the horizon on one of the one-third lines (Figure 3-13). Any of these suggestions will add a great deal of interest to the photo by breaking up its boring sameness and/or giving the feeling of holding the scene together. (Important: Use the technique of framing the subject in any type of photo, not just scenics.)

Figure 3-11

Figure 3-12

Figure 3-13

SELECTIVE FOCUS

During the discussions on framing and background, I have hinted at the use of another tool of photographic composition—selective focus. With this technique, you apply what you have learned about depth of field. Some photos seem best with sharp focus running from the framing objects in the foreground to the scenic background, thus requiring the largest possible amount of depth of field (Figure 3-14). Photographer Ansel Adams is a master of this technique, definitely meriting your study. In other photos, a shallow depth of field is most effective. An out-of-focus foreground object framing a well-focused subject (Figure 3-15) or an in-focus foreground subject with an out-of-focus background (Figure 3-16) put this technique to good use.

Figure 3-14

35

Figure 3-15

Figure 3-16

SHAPE THEMES

Photos can also be well composed without the use of framing or depth-of-field techniques, if they have an overall "shape" theme in them. If your photo can be reduced to a simple, overall pattern such as a letter or geometric shape, the picture can create a well-composed feeling. Examples: (1) The shoreline of a charming pond pulls away from you in a gentle "S" or "C" shape; (2) A photo is split diagonally into two right triangles by its large triangular light and dark (or foreground and background) sections (Figure 3-17); (3) An S-shaped road draws your eyes to an attractive, low building (Figure 3-18).

If you use the techniques suggested in this chapter, your photos will gain strength and appeal. Use these methods as though they were rules until you have mastered them. Once these techniques have helped you develop an eye for a good picture, they have served their purpose and can be cast off. Your eye will then begin telling you that it sees a good photo, even though it breaks all the rules discussed in this chapter (Figure 3-19). When you reach this level of adeptness, you should trust your eye—there is a very good chance that it has seen an outstanding photographic possibility.

Use the techniques presented in this chapter, but do not become their slave—dare *not* to use them, also.

A final suggestion. Start saving any interesting photos that you find in magazines and photographic annuals. Try to figure out what it is that makes each photo worth your attention and what techniques the photographer used to create the picture. You will find some you like for no apparent reason and some you detest even though they may follow the rules. Hopefully, this will help discipline your eye so that you may make better, composed photos more consistently and easily.

Figure 3-17

Figure 3-18

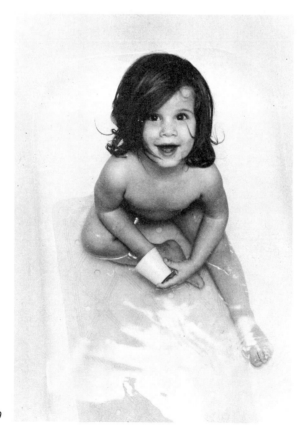

Figure 3-19

4

LIGHTING

Light is very special. Not only does it make the entire photographic process possible, but if carefully observed and properly used, it can be the difference between a beautiful, exciting photo or a trite, boring snapshot.

Begin concerning yourself with light direction (the direction that light strikes the photo's subject in relation to the camera). An overwhelmingly large percentage of photos are of subjects that are lighted from the front. In other words, the camera is pointed at the portion of the subject that is directly in the light (Figure 4-1).

BACKLIGHTING

For interesting variations, you may use backlighting or sidelighting. A subject is backlighted if the light is coming from the opposite side of the subject than the camera (Figure 4-2). Backlighting often lends a moody or sentimental feeling to photos (Figure 4-3), but not without causing some exposure problems. Backlighted subjects are normally ringed by surroundings much brighter than themselves. In order to properly expose a backlighted subject, you should employ one of the following techniques.

(1) Using a reflected-light meter (hand-held or one built into a camera), measure the light reflected from just the subject, or from an 18% gray card in the subject's position.

(2) Using an incident-light meter, aim the meter's light-collecting hemisphere at the camera from the subject's position.

(3) Meter the whole scene, then open the aperture one, two, or three stops more than indicated by your meter, depending on how bright the backlighting is—I'm sorry I can't be more specific. You will have to guess. Then "bracket" the exposure by shooting several exposures—one at the exposure value you have scientifically guessed, one more at the exposure value (EV) plus one f/stop, one at EV plus two f/stops, one at EV minus one f/stop, and one at EV minus two f/stops. This should insure at least one properly exposed photo. Make note of which exposure worked—by doing so you will eventually be able to make more accurate exposure estimates.

Any one of the above methods will guarantee success in exposing backlighted subjects.

Figure 4-1

Figure 4-2

Figure 4-3

SIDELIGHTING

When the light source is to the side of the subject (90 degrees from the camera-to-subject axis), the subject is sidelighted (Figure 4-4). Sidelighting can add strength, depth, interest, or tone to a photo, as in the man's portrait, Figure 4-5. It can also add an almost palpable texture, as in Figure 4-6. Unlike backlighting, there is no need to make any exposure compensation. Sidelighted subjects may be exposed normally.

Light intensity should always be considered when taking pictures. Certain subjects, such as the barn boards in Figure 4-6, just beg for high intensity sidelighting. Outdoors, high intensity light is available on any cloudless day, and will give its maximum effect in the early morning or late afternoon. Shadows at these times are at their longest and blackest, and create the illusion of three dimensions within a two-dimensional photo.

Figure 4-4

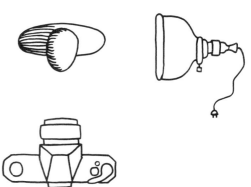

Figure 4-5

Figure 4-6

43

HARSH LIGHTING

While strong, harsh lighting is quite effective for creating super-real textures and fascinating scenics, normally it should not be used for portraiture. Such lighting accentuates every wrinkle, crease, and blemish and forces the model to squint. When outdoors, you can avoid intense light and its concommitant harsh shadows by placing the subject in open shade or by shooting on a cloudy or overcast day. If the shade is a little too dark, more light can be added by reflecting sunlight from a sheet of white poster board onto the subject.

When indoors, you can produce harsh light by using a strong, point-source light. Point-source light refers to illumination from a relatively compact or distant light that is aimed directly at the subject. Such lighting can be obtained from nearly any incandescent lamp, flashgun, or even candles (Figure 4-7).

At times, harsh light will be undesirable indoors. To soften its intensity, you must diffuse the light. This can be accomplished by either of the following methods.

(1) Reflect light onto the subject by aiming it at a light-colored wall, ceiling, or poster board. Keep redirecting the light until the desired effect is reached. This process is commonly referred to as "bounce light," a term that conjures up thoughts of shattered light bulbs.

(2) Alternately, you can diffuse the light through a translucent object, such as paper, cloth, or milk-colored glass, or plastic.

Do not use either of these techniques with color film, unless the reflective surface or diffusing medium is white. Otherwise, the entire photo will be tinted the same color as the reflective surface or diffusing medium.

Figure 4-7

ARTIFICIAL LIGHTING

There will be times when there will not be enough light available to photograph some object that is fairly close to the camera (within about 30 feet or 10 meters). The two most likely solutions are to shoot an exposure of several seconds or minutes (often inconvenient when photographing living beings), or to use a flash unit.

Flash and Strobe Units

An electronic flash unit, or "strobe" (one that stores electricity in a capacitor capable of discharging it in a tiny fraction of a second), will probably be your choice. For most purposes, a unit that has a list price of about $25 will be sufficient. Electronic flashguns are powered by penlight batteries, rechargeable, nickel-cadmium batteries, and/or regular AC power. For proper exposure under normal use, follow the instructions that come with the strobe. Alternately, you may use an automatic exposure-control strobe or a conventional flashbulb in a flashgun. The auto-strobes are more expensive than standard strobes. Flashbulbs are initially cheaper but can be used only once. Whatever you choose will be a trade-off between cost and convenience.

If your camera has a focal-plane shutter, the maximum shutter speed that you will be able to use with electronic flash will most likely be 1/60 sec. or possibly 1/80 or 1/125 sec., depending upon the camera model. Check your camera's instructions for its maximum, electronic flash-synchronization speed. Speeds faster than those recommended will produce blank, imageless frames of film or frames that are partially blank.

My favorite type of low-cost flash is the penlight, cell-powered unit. As long as you have a spare set of batteries, you won't lose the time needed to recharge the nickel-cadmium units. The best batteries for the penlight-powered flash are the alkaline variety, such as Eveready's Energizers or Mallory's Duracells. These will last much longer than standard batteries. Their life can be extended even further if you "charge" your flash unit (until the "ready" light comes on) before each shooting session with cheap, standard batteries.

Automatic Exposure Flash

Standard electronic flash units are relatively small and convenient, but they require the user to compute proper exposure. Convenience is increased with the use of an automatic, exposure-controlled flash. Such units have photoelectric eyes that read the light flashed onto the subject and determine the duration of the flash for sufficient illumination.

An improved automatic exposure flash has recently appeared that overcomes some of the weaknesses of electronic flash. Most electronic flash units take anywhere from 8 to 30 seconds to recycle to full power between flashes. These units usually wear out their batteries fairly quickly. The new type unit, though, usually called a thyrister-controlled, automatic flash, can recycle quickly and can obtain many times more flashes than nonthyrister units. They are expensive but awfully nice.

Reducing Shadows

Any of these powerful, little light sources will cause harsh shadows in much the same manner as direct sunlight. To avoid the shadows, try one of the following four suggestions.

The first method is to cover the face of the flash unit with one layer of a white handkerchief, fastening it on with a rubber band (Figure 4-8). You will have to open the aperture one stop more (such as f/4 to f/2.8) than the unit's calculator suggests so that you can make up for the light absorbed by the handkerchief. If more diffusion is necessary, you will have to experiment with larger apertures and more layers of cloth.

The second method, which is quite similar to the first, also involves the attachment of a translucent object to an electronic flash unit. Tape a piece of white paper over the lens of the flash unit so that the paper forms a convex crescent (Figure 4-9). Expose by opening the aperture one stop more than suggested on the flash unit's calculator.

The third method is to bounce the illumination of the flash onto your subject. To compute the proper aperture, estimate the sum of the distances between the flash unit and the reflective surface and between the reflective surface and the subject (Figure 4-10). Use this total distance, with the flash unit's computing table, to arrive at the suggested aperture, and then open up one additional stop. Example: The distance from the flash to the reflective surface is six feet; and the distance from the reflective surface to your subject is four feet. Use the total distance, ten feet, as the flash to subject distance. Shoot the picture while aiming the flash at the reflective surface.

The Larson Company markets a special gadget designed for bounce-flash use. Called "Reflectasol," it consists of a silvered umbrella with a system of light clamps and stands. Flash units are aimed into the Reflectasol which in turn acts as a diffusion-reflection device. Consider buying one if you have enough extra cash in your photography budget.

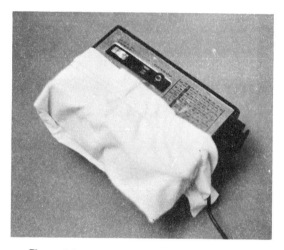

Figure 4-8

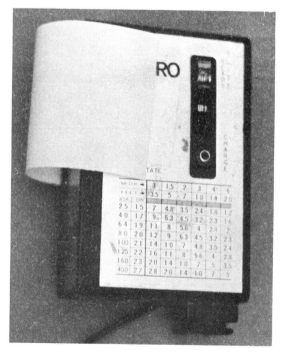

Figure 4-9

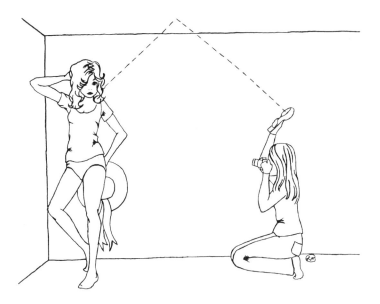

Figure 4-10

The fourth method of reducing harsh shadows due to strong flash illumination is technically fascinating but relatively expensive. It involves the use of an automatic exposure flash unit that is specifically designed to be used for effortless bounce illumination. Strobes of this type feature an electronic-eye control that remains pointed at the subject regardless of where the flash itself is aimed. The strobe's circuitry does all the computing for you—the ultimate in convenience.

Should you decide to go all the way and buy a thyrister-controlled, automatic strobe that can measure bounce light, be sure to select one that is powerful enough to overcome the light loss inherent to the bounce-flash technique. Effective illumination will be cut in half by being diffused off a matte-surfaced reflector, and it will be further reduced by the increased flash to subject distance. Therefore, buy a thyrister-controlled, auto-strobe with a guide number (analogous to horsepower rating for a car) of at least 50 for Kodachrome II film, ASA 25. Much smaller guide numbers are satisfactory if you don't intend to do much bounce-flash work.

A weakness of nearly all flash units is that their on-off switches have a nasty habit of turning themselves on as soon as you pack the unit into a camera bag or suitcase. This results in drained batteries. You can overcome this weakness by either taping the switch in the off position or by packing the flash unit away with its batteries removed.

47

STUDIO LIGHTING

Our discussion on lighting would not be complete without an introduction to multi-source illumination and special effects.

Most studio lighting, whether fashion, product, or portrait photography, involves the use of three or four light sources. The strongest of the four light sources, called the "main light," is usually positioned just to the side of and somewhat higher than the camera and pointed at the subject (Part A of Figure 4-11). Ideally, the angle formed between the main light, subject, and camera should be about 45 degrees. The shadows thrown by the main light point diagonally downward, very much resembling the familiar shadow angle caused by sunlight—normally a pleasing effect.

The second light, termed "fill light," is positioned on the other side of the camera, at about the same height as the camera and pointing at the subject (Part B of Figure 4-11). The fill light will soften shadows cast by the main light and reduce the overall contrast between the left and right sides of the subject. Ideally, for portraiture, when both the main and fill lights are turned on, the main-lighted side of the subject should be one or two f/stops brighter than the fill-lighted side. This difference in illumination can be measured easily with any light meter and adjusted by varying the wattage of the lamps as well as the distance between the lights and subject.

The third light is used to produce highlights at the top of the subject, and in portraiture, is logically referred to as a "hair light." The hair light is positioned high, behind the subject, off to one side, and aimed at the top rear of the subject (Part C of Figure 4-11). Be careful not to allow illumination from the hair light to spill over onto the front of the subject, or it will change the light balance. Hair light should only rim the top of the subject with light.

The fourth light is positioned low, behind the subject, and aimed upward at the background (Part D of Figure 4-11). This light is optional and should be used only when an illuminated background is desired.

The foregoing is merely a starting point. Light intensities and subject and light positions can be varied according to need or taste. Should you decide to attempt studio lighting, you can purchase the necessary photoflood bulbs, sockets, reflectors, and light stands or clamps for a small sum of money (below $50) at any well-stocked camera store.

Figure 4-11

Figure 4-12

SPECIAL EFFECTS LIGHTING

Having covered most of the basics of photographic lighting, I will now try to stimulate your imagination by citing some ways in which lighting can be used to achieve special effects.

Glass and crystal objects can become stunning photographic subjects with hardly any effort on the part of the photographer. Pictures like Figure 4-12 are made by strongly lighting the glassware from either the side or bottom. If you decide to light from beneath the glassware, place the object on a translucent or transparent base material.

It is fairly simple to simulate pictures that are seemingly impossible to expose properly (Figure 4-13). If, for instance, you wished to photograph a scene that was lighted only by a fireplace or a jack-o-lantern, the normal routine would be to make a time exposure—most difficult if a living person or other animated object is to be in the photo. Instead of using fire or candlelight, place a small electronic flash unit in the fireplace (unlit!) or in the jack-o-lantern, facing outward from the location where the fire or candle should be. Connect an electronic flash unit extension cord between the flash and camera. Such extension cords can be found in most camera stores. Buy one that will be long enough. To compute exposure, use the flash to subject distance.

Start training yourself to be observant and to notice what effect light has on different objects. Make note of how light direction, intensity, and shadow quality can change the appearance of your subject matter. Training your eye in this manner will help you create better photographs.

Figure 4-13

5

LENSES AND FILTERS

All of the photographic techniques discussed so far can be used with whatever lens-camera combination you may try. With the addition of different lenses, you can achieve even more dramatic effects using the same techniques, thereby adding new picture-making capabilities to your repertoire. It is for this reason that I urged you to buy a camera that features lens interchangeability in Chapter 1.

Lenses can be categorized as normal, wide-angle, or telephoto and differ in two ways—angle of view and apparent image size. Variations of apparent image size and angle of view can be seen in Figures 5-1 through 5-5.

The normal lens is so called because the view you see through it is about the same as what you see with the naked eye. It is probably the lens that came with your camera (Figure 5-2).

Figure 5-1

Figure 5-2

Figure 5-3

Figure 5-4

Figure 5-5

WIDE-ANGLE LENSES

The wide-angle lens is so called because what you see through it encompasses a wider angle of view than what you see through the normal lens. Also, the objects that you see through a wide-angle lens will appear smaller than they do through a normal lens. In other words, the view through a wide-angle lens is similar to the view through a normal lens moved further away from the subject (Figure 5-1).

A wide-angle lens produces three useful effects. First, because a wide-angle lens sees a wider angle than a normal lens, it is capable of including more of a particular scene when there is not enough room for the photographer to step back. This is how advertising photographers are able to shoot interiors of cars and small rooms (Figure 5-6). Second, at a given distance from your subject, a wide-angle lens will have a greater depth of field than a normal lens (depth of field is that area in a photo in

front of and beyond the subject that appears to be in focus). Third, a wide-angle lens will seem to distort a picture in an interesting way. That is, objects will appear to diminish into the distance more than they actually do. (A car's interior will look roomier than it really is—another reason why the advertising photographer uses a wide-angle lens for auto interiors.) If an object is close to a wide-angle lens, it will look gigantic in front of its rapidly diminishing background (Figure 5-7).

Wide-angle lenses tend to range from mildly wide (35mm focal length) to super "fisheye" lenses that produce pictures that look like the reflection on a mirrored globe or the back of a spoon. If your budget will allow the purchase of only one wide-angle lens, a 28mm probably would be your best choice. It is significantly wider than a 35mm lens but still not so wide that its use is severely limited.

Figure 5-6

TELEPHOTO LENSES

Telephoto lenses are much akin to small, precise telescopes. They have a smaller angle of view and yield a larger image than a normal lens. Telephotos have the ability of viewing distant objects as though they were up close (Figures 5-3 through 5-5).

There are qualities that make a telephoto lens rather nice to have. First, it is possible to create an extremely shallow depth of field with a telephoto lens. Second, opposite to a wide-angle lens, which seems to stretch out perspective, a telephoto seems to compress perspective (those sunset photos with an immense sun behind the silhouetted subject, for example). Third, a telephoto allows you to photograph your subject from a long distance. A lens in the 135-200mm range (2½ to 4 times "normal") is great for getting those shots of people mentioned in Chapter 3, allowing you to keep out of their way. A 200mm lens or larger is ideal at the beach, if you are too shy to ask permission to photograph the girls. If the subject is shy, as is most wildlife, this size lens is your choice. Lenses in the 80-120mm range are the best ones for portraiture. They allow you to fill the camera's viewfinder with your subject, without being too close for comfort.

Some cautions should be observed when using telephoto lenses. (1) Unless stopped down fairly far, telephotos have a *shallow* depth of field. (2) The weight of some of the larger lenses might damage lens mounts if the lens itself is not supported. (3) The larger the lens, the more it will magnify any shake or vibration of the camera. Therefore, you will need to select a faster shutter speed, when using a telephoto with only hand support. The following table should help you choose minimum shutter speeds for hand-held use.

Focal length (lens size)	Minimum shutter speed (hand-held)
50mm	1/30 sec.
100mm	1/60 sec.
200mm	1/125 sec.
400mm	1/250 sec.

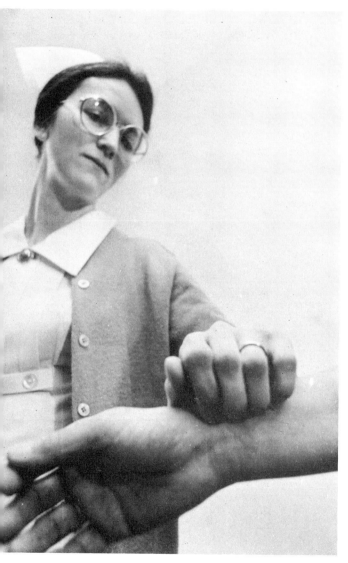

Figure 5-7

TELE-EXTENDERS

A wonderfully cheap way of increasing your collection of lenses is with the purchase of a "tele-extender." It attaches to a camera between the lens and body, and multiplies the focal length by two or three times, depending on whether it is a 2x or 3x extender, respectively. If you owned only the 50mm and 135mm lenses, the addition of a 2x extender would effectively give you a 100mm (2 x 50mm) and a 270mm (2 x 135mm) lens. As a bonus, tele-extenders will give you semi close-up capability. Tele-extenders still allow you to focus your lens as close as it normally can be focused without a tele-extender interposed between the lens and the camera. Thus, it doubles or triples image size, depending on whether a

2x or 3x tele-extender is used (Figures 5-8 and 5-9). You don't get something for nothing, though. Tele-extenders do not allow quite as fine picture quality as regular lenses; nor do they allow as much light to reach the film. Extenders of 2x magnification cut down the amount of light by the equivalent of 2 f/stops and extenders of 3x magnification by the equivalent of 3 f/stops. If you use a 2x and 3x tele-extender simultaneously, the resulting increase in focal length will be 6x, and the effective maximum amount of light reaching the film will be reduced by 6 f/stops. For example, a 50mm f/1.4 lens, when attached to a 2x and 3x tele-extender will become a 300mm lens with a maximum effective amount of light equal to f/11 passing through it.

Figure 5-8

Figure 5-9

ZOOM LENSES

Zoom lenses have come into universal use in television and motion picture production, but they have not gained wide popularity in still photography. This is because zoom lenses are expensive, and with a few exceptions, are not capable of producing results as good as fixed focal-length lenses. (Zoom lenses have variable focal lengths. An 85-205mm zoom lens can be set for any of the 121 focal lengths within its range.) Zoom lenses are immensely convenient and worth your consideration. One reason to buy a zoom lens is that it can be used with the utmost speed. It is much quicker to change focal-length settings on a zoom lens than it is to remove one lens from your camera and attach another. One zoom lens is lighter and less bulky than the two or more lenses within its focal-length range that a photographer may own, and consequently, will save weight and space when traveling.

Most manufacturers of top, expensive cameras make good zoom lenses that are sold at high prices. Some zooms that have received fine critical ratings, but are relatively inexpensive, are the Vivitar 55-135mm, the Lentar 80-200mm, and the Vivitar Series 1 70-210mm lenses. By now there may be others available that are both inexpensive and of exceptional quality. Check the lens and camera test sections of *Camera 35*, *Modern Photography*, and *Popular Photography* magazines for the latest reviews of zoom lenses.

If you do buy a zoom lens, be sure to focus it at its maximum focal length (its most telescopic setting) and then "zoom" to the size you want. This will produce the best results.

Zoom lenses offer more than just convenience in that they can also be used to make startlingly unusual color or black-and-white photos. With a zoom lens attached, mount the camera on a sturdy tripod. Focus and compose. Then, check and adjust the exposure so that a shutter speed of 1/4 sec. or slower is set on the shutter-speed scale. Adjust the lens to its maximum or minimum focal length. Now gingerly press the shutter release and quickly zoom the lens all the way to its opposite focal length. (For example, if you are using an 85-205mm lens that was set to its 205mm focal length, quickly zoom to the 85mm focal length.) To achieve the proper effect of a subject surrounded by converging streaks, you must do all of the zooming during the time the shutter remains open. Also, try two different exposures: one zooming from the maximum to the minimum focal length, and one zooming from the minimum to the maximum focal length.

AUTOMATIC AND PRESET LENSES

All the lenses available today have either an "automatic" or "preset" diaphragm, and are called automatic or preset lenses. The diaphragm of an automatic lens will remain all the way open until you depress the shutter-release button, then a linkage in your camera will cause the aperture to close down to the f/stop that you set on the lens. Microseconds later, the shutter will open and close, and the diaphragm will snap back to maximum opening.

With a preset lens, you also start by choosing an f/stop setting. When you are ready to take a picture, you must twist another control ring as far as it will go. This will close down the aperture to the f/stop you selected earlier. Now you can go ahead and press the shutter release.

From these two descriptions, you can see that the automatic lens is considerably quicker, easier, and more convenient to use than a preset lens. But an automatic lens requires linkages and springs not needed in a preset lens and is, therefore, more expensive than a preset. If your budget allows, hang the expense for any lens with a focal length longer than 18mm and shorter than 300mm—the convenience outweighs the cost. With most lenses beyond these extremes, the cost to convenience ratio quickly becomes less favorable.

Figure 5-10

LENS SHADES

No matter what lens or lenses you have, one of the most valuable accessories you can buy is a lens hood or sunshade. A sunshade will improve picture quality, from a technical point of view, by reducing "flare" or surface reflections on the lens. My favorite type of lens shade is the collapsible rubber hood that screws into the front end of the lens (Figure 5-10).

FILTERS

A second useful accessory is the photographic filter—a precision ground and dyed piece of colored glass or a colored gelatin. Filters are intended to be used for two purposes: correction and special effects. Correction filters help restore natural tones (for black-and-white film) and colors (for color film) to pictures. Special-effects filters make exaggerated or unnatural effects, tones, and colors possible.

Some photographers use photographic filters for virtually all of their pictures, while other photographers seldom, if ever, use them. It is possible for you to produce excellent photos without ever employing filters, but there are certain instances when they are useful.

Filters are usually attached to the front of lenses by means of screw threads. All lenses are not of the same diameter. Hence, you should consult the specifications of a lens to see what diameter "accessories" can be purchased for proper fit.

In black-and-white photography, there are three general rules for the use of filters.

1. Objects will be lightened by filters of similar color. For example, a blue sky photographed through a blue filter will photograph lighter than without the filter.

2. Objects will be darkened by filters of complementary or near complementary color. For example, a blue sky photographed through an orange filter will photograph darker than without the filter.

3. Use filters only when some benefits can be realized. Anything placed between the subject and film will somehow affect the final image. When filters are interposed to achieve an effect, the results should be pleasing. But if filters are employed when not needed, they may deteriorate the final image. For example, a strongly backlighted scene photographed through a filter may become "muddied" by light refracting and reflecting in the filter's glass (this phenomenon is called flare). Further, filters will absorb some light, thus requiring you to increase exposure.

Referring to Figures 5-11 through 5-15, we can graphically see the effects of filters. Filters are most often employed to make clouds stand out better in a black-and-white picture (Figure 5-16). This is accomplished by darkening the surrounding blue sky with a filter of a complementary color to blue, such as yellow, orange, or red. The desired effect will work only when photographing a partially overcast sky.

For most purposes, you may determine proper exposure directly through a filter. That is, using the camera's through-the-lens light meter, determine exposure with a filter attached to the lens. This may cause slight errors in exposure, due to the fact that most light meters are more sensitive to certain colors of light. Most commonly, meters are very sensitive to colors toward the low end of the light spectrum (red/orange/yellow) and less sensitive to colors toward the high end of the light spectrum (blue/violet). Thus, photographs taken through yellow filters will often be somewhat overexposed, and photographs taken through blue filters will often be somewhat underexposed.

Figure 5-11

5-12

Figure 5-13

Figure 5-14

Figure 5-15

61

Figure 5-16

Filter Factors

In most cases, exposure differences are negligible. However, high-speed color films, such as Kodak High Speed Ektachrome or GAF 200 and 500, tend to be rather unforgiving of exposure errors. When using filters with these films, it would be best if you would determine exposure in the following manner. First, determine what would be the proper exposure without a filter attached to the camera. Use the camera's meter (or a hand-held meter) just as you learned in Chapter 2. Then, compute the corrected exposure for the filter you intend to use. To compute this value, start by locating the "filter-factor" number, which is normally engraved on the metal rim of the filter. Typically, a filter factor may be marked as 2x, 3x, 4x, 5x, 6x, or 8x. This refers to two times, three times, four times, five times, six times, or eight times the normal exposure. In Chapter 2, you learned that increasing the aperture by one f/stop or decreasing the shutter speed by one setting will double the exposure. Therefore, a filter factor of 2x (twice normal exposure) can be figured in by opening the aperture one stop more than indicated by the exposure meter. Similarly, 3x requires a $1^1/_2$-stop increase, 4x requires a 2-stop increase, 5x requires a $2^1/_3$-stop increase, 6x requires a $2^1/_2$-stop increase, and 8x requires a 3-stop increase of exposure.

If the above explanation has confused you, refer to the following table in order to compute exposure with filters.

Filter Factor	f/Stop Increases of Exposure
2x	1 stop
3x	$1^1/_2$ stops
4x	2 stops
5x	$2^1/_3$ stops
6x	$2^1/_2$ stops
8x	3 stops

As mentioned before, filters for color photography are used to correct a color imbalance or to provide a special effect. Different light sources are composed of dissimilar colors, and therefore, cause an overall tint to be recorded on the film. Normally, we are not able to detect these differences in light because the brain compensates for color changes. Film cannot perform such compensations. Hence, the need for filters or different films.

Daylight and Tungsten Films

Film manufacturers make film balanced for either "daylight" (outdoor) or the light of ordinary tungsten filament bulbs (indoor). Daylight film will give true color rendition in daylight, when using almost any electronic flash unit or when using blue, coated flashbulbs. Be careful early and late in the day, though. When the sun is near the horizon, light tends toward the reds, oranges, and yellows. Tungsten light-balanced film will give true color rendition only with light of the same color as the light given off by a tungsten-filament bulb. There are two different light-value tungsten films manufactured, because there are two different values of tungsten lamps manufactured.

Daylight color film may be used indoors if you use a daylight-balanced flash or if you shoot through a color-compensation filter. If the tungsten light has a color value (or color temperature) of 3200 K (this figure is often inscribed on photoflood lamps), the proper filter to use is a number 80A. If the light source has a color temperature of 3400 K, the proper filter to use is a number 80B. The suggested filters are the ones to use for the most accurate color correction, but for most purposes, either filter will do for either lamp (both filters are similar shades of blue).

In order to use indoor, or tungsten, film in a daylight environment, you must use an orange number 85 or 85B filter. The following chart will help you select the proper filter.

Light Source	Daylight	Tungsten A 3200 K	Tungsten B 3400 K
Daylight	No filter	Filter 85	Filter 85B
3200 K	Filter 80A	No Filter	No Filter
3400 K	Filter 80B	No Filter	No Filter

Color Photos

Sometimes color photos are so realistic that they require virtually no imagination on the part of the viewer to interpret what he sees. Super-real color photos of this kind can actually be dull. A simple and effective way to overcome the "color-photo dulls" is to use filters that tint the photo unreal colors. Spiratone, Inc., markets a group of filters called "Vibracolor," which have been manufactured specifically to meet this need. If you want to try something different with your color photos, experiment with Vibracolor filters.

There are several filters available that can be used for both color and black-and-white photography. One such filter, a neutral density filter, has no effect on the photographic process other than to reduce the amount of light that reaches the film. This provides another way to control exposure, allowing the photographer to choose otherwise impossible f/stop–shutter-speed combinations.

A polarizing filter is constructed in such a way as to allow you to rotate it on the end of your lens. By rotating it, you can reduce the glare from reflections employing the same principle that is used for Polaroid sunglasses. A second benefit of polarizing filters is that they will darken blue skies. Check your camera's manual to see how you should expose when using a polarizing filter.

Special-Effects Filters

The remaining color and black-and-white filters are intended for use for special effects. One, which is composed of a piece of screen mounted in a filter holder, produces a star-like phenomenon at each strong light source or bright reflection, as in Figure 5-17. This effect is often used in television productions. Ask for either a cross-screen or star-effect filter, if you decide to buy one.

A fog-effect filter is one that simulates fog by partially diffusing the light that passes through it. There are other special-effects filters marketed that can do such things as produce multiple images or allow you to sharply focus on a very close-up object while clearly resolving a more distant background. The possibilities for the creative use of filters are almost boundless, limited only by the imagination.

It would be wise for you to buy either a "skylight" (1A) or "ultraviolet" (UV) filter for each lens that you own and use regularly. If you keep one attached to the front of your lens, it will help protect the lens from curious fingers and raucous beer parties. The UV filter will not affect color pictures in any way, and neither filter will affect black-and-white pictures.

This picture is pleasing since basic compositional rules have been followed. This photo would have been far less interesting if the steeple stood alone against the sky without being framed by the tree limbs. Taken with 55mm lens, f/8, 1/125 sec. on Ektachrome film.

(Left) Selective focus and color on a drab background rivet one's attention to the subject. This photo is in a vertical format because standing people are usually taller than they are wide. A 210mm zoom lens was used at f/3.5, 1/250 sec., Fujichrome film. (Below) The dominant colors in this picture, though devoid of vivid tone, still seem to glow. This is because (1) the colors stand out against a drab background; and (2) overcast or shaded conditions tend to produce stronger color. Notice how the 28mm wide-angle lens adds depth to the scene. Taken at f/8, 1/30 sec. on Agfachrome film.

Color can add a new, creative dimension to your photos. But BEWARE! Too many colors can produce a boring, amateurish snapshot. Try limiting the colors as shown here. A 55mm lens was used at f/5.6, 1/60 sec., Fujichrome film.

(Left) Natural light takes on a mystical quality at dusk. To capture such quality on film in the morning, expose for one to two minutes after the light looks most exciting. In the evening, expose for one to two minutes before the magic moment. Taken with a 150mm zoom lens, at f/3.5, 1/125 sec. on Fujichrome film. (Below) Proper exposure is most critical with color film. Whenever possible, use the gray card metering technique discussed in Chapter 2. For this photo, I had to guess its exposure because the humid salt air disabled my light meter. I "bracketed" by shooting several exposures using a half-stop difference for each attempt. Once developed, I discovered that the best photo had received a one-second exposure at f/1.8 on Agfachrome film.

Figure 5-17

EQUIPMENT CARE

Filters and lenses are precision manufactured goods that deserve the best care possible. Any dirt, dust, soil, grease, and the like, that contact their glass surfaces should be removed both to protect the lens and to prevent unnecessary degrading of picture quality. Dust can best be removed with a blast of air from a blower brush or syringe (Figure 5-18). Do not substitute your own breath for a blower brush. Invariably, the moment you want to blow just air from your mouth, a significant amount of moisture will decide to come along for the ride. More stubborn dirt, grease, and fingerprints can be removed with a drop of lens cleaning solution and careful wiping with a lens tissue. Do not rub hard, or you may scratch the glass.

Figure 5-18

FOCAL LENGTH

A difficult concept to comprehend is focal length. It is included here only for those curious enough to want to learn it. If you are not interested, you may skip ahead to the next chapter.

Focal length refers to the distance between the optical center of a lens and the film, while the lens is focused on infinity.

Focal length will determine image size. That is, different size (focal-length) lenses will cause your subject to appear different sizes on the film. The normal lens (around 50mm using a 35mm camera) will produce an image on the film that is about the same size as the subject appears to be from your vantage point, using the naked eye. If you double the focal length to 100mm (telephoto), the image size will double. If you halve the focal length, to 25mm (wide-angle), the image will be reduced to one-half the size you see with the naked eye. This, as you remember from the beginning of this chapter, is one of the differences between lenses of different focal lengths—apparent image size.

Angle of View

Angle of view varies inversely to the image size. As the image size increases, the image fills more and more of the film, excluding other objects from the frame of film —in effect, narrowing the angle of view on the film. The following chart lists angles of view for several, common, lens focal lengths.

Focal length in mm	Wide-angle			Normal		Telephoto			
	21	28	35	50	55	90	105	135	200
Angle of view in degrees	91	76	63	46	43	27	23	18	12

Figures 5-1 through 5-5 graphically depict these differences.

If you have survived this final harangue, congratulations are in order. Now let's develop the pictures you have taken.

6

FILM AND DEVELOPMENT

At the risk of offending the "motherhood, flag, and apple pie" set, I will now try to convince you to spurn that great American tradition of leaving all your film at a drugstore for processing. This chapter will deal with films and their development. (Have your first rolls of film processed professionally. This way you can be assured that you are using your camera properly before in-troducing the new variable of home developing.)

Black-and-white film consists of a clear, plastic-base material and a light-sensitive, silver compound suspended in a gelatin and applied to the base. Variations in this compound will cause different films to have different properties. Some of these properties are speed, graininess, and contrast.

FILM SPEED

Speed is the relative sensitivity of a film to light. "Fast" films are more sensitive to light than "slow" films, and therefore, can be used when there is less light available. Films are laboratory tested to arrive at ASA and DIN speed ratings (see Chap. 2). The higher the number, the faster the film. One would assume that the best film to use would be the fastest one, but other factors have to be considered, such as graininess.

FILM GRAININESS

If you looked at a negative through a microscope, you would see that the images are formed by different sized clumps of grains, which may be visible once a photo is enlarged. Generally, larger grain clumps are more sensitive to light than smaller ones. Therefore, most fast films, which have the larger, more sensitive grains, will be grainier than slow films. Visible grain is usually considered objectionable, but there are instances when grain will contribute to the overall effect of a composition (Figure 6-1).

Figure 6-1

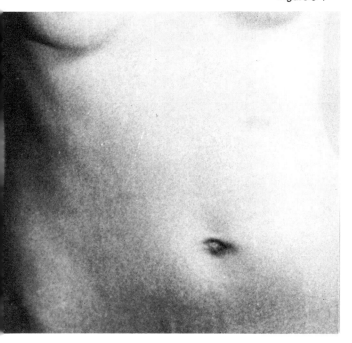

FILM CONTRAST

Contrast in a film is the difference between the lightest and darkest tones that can be produced on it. Generally, the slower the film, the more contrast is possible.

Some common black-and-white films are as follows:

Kodak Panatomic X: Slow ASA 32, *very* fine grain.

H & W Control VTE Pan: Moderate ASA 80, *ultra*-fine grain.

Kodak Plus-X: Moderate ASA 125, fine grain.

Kodak Tri-X: Fast ASA 400, moderate grain.

Color films vary as to speed and color balance. Several good color-slide films are listed below.

Kodachrome II: Slow ASA 25, superb color, resolution, color balance.

Agfachrome 64: Moderate ASA 64, vibrant warm colors, subtly tinted toward red.

Kodak Ektachrome: Moderate ASA 64, cool colors, subtly tinted toward blue.

Fujichrome R-100: Fast ASA 100, warm colors, subtly tinted toward red, realistic tones in fluorescent lighting.

Kodak High Speed Ektachrome: Fast ASA 160, cool colors, subtly tinted toward blue.

GAF 200 and 500: Very fast ASA 200 and 500, respectively, warm colors subtly tinted toward red, GAF 200 only available in 20-exposure cartridges for 35mm.

DEVELOPING BLACK-AND-WHITE FILM

In order to see the images recorded on film, you must develop it. Before you begin, remember: strictly follow the cardinal rules of developing. Cleanliness is the foremost rule. Always keep your equipment, chemicals, and work areas spotlessly clean. Dust is the worst enemy of any photographer and can quickly ruin your greatest efforts. Adherence to directions is the second mandate. Manufacturers of photographic film, chemicals, and equipment have spent countless hours of testing to arrive at the best possible methods of using their products. Trust them. They have no reason to deceive you. In fact, if they want your repeated patronage, they must properly describe the use of their goods. The third rule of developing is absolute consistency. There are so many factors that can vary in the photographic process that unless as many variables as possible are controlled, you may seldom achieve acceptable results. Therefore, always do all the steps of film development in the same manner, without varying technique. (This particular "never" can be varied once you graduate to an advanced status and begin experimenting with different methods to produce effects.)

Developing Needs

The first thing you will need in order to develop film is an absolutely dark place. A closet with towels stuffed in the cracks around the door will do nicely. You spend only one or two minutes in the closet, because most of the developing process can be done in daylight.

The second item you will need is a developing tank. You probably will be advised to buy a stainless steel tank. Wait before taking this advice. Although stainless steel tanks are nearly indestructible and allow rapid temperature change, they have several faults. Whenever you want the top off, it gets stuck, and whenever you want the top on, it falls off. Stainless steel tanks are usually far more expensive than other types and tend to leak at least as much. Furthermore, its film reels are more difficult to load than the reels that come with plastic tanks.

Plastic tanks range from the very inexpensive, but adequate, Yankee tanks to the deluxe tanks made by Paterson—my personal favorite. Any of these will serve you well, provided it has either a "self-loading" reel or one that is easy for you to load. Ask the camera salesman to demonstrate tanks and reels for you. Try them yourself to make sure that you will be able, after practicing, to load them in total darkness. If you are unable to load any of the available reels, ask the salesman to let you try an "apron" type load (he will know what you mean).

Loading Your Tank

Practice loading your developing tank with some unexposed film, first watching what you are doing, then with your eyes closed, and finally, in total darkness. Be sure that during your practice you form the habit of handling film only by its edges. Fingerprints can stain the film permanently. Once you are confident that you can properly load film into the tank, take the tank, exposed film, a pair of scissors, and a bottle opener into your "dark place." Put the tank, its top and reel separated, in front of you, and stick the bottle opener, film, and scissors in your pockets. Thoroughly darken the area. Open the film cartridge by using the bottle opener to pry off the flat end of the cartridge. Take the film out of the cartridge and cut off the uneven leader portion of the film. Next, load the film onto the reel

until you reach the end attached to the spool. Cut the film off about one-half to one iinch away from the spool, and load the rest of the film onto the reel. Now put the reel into the tank (right side up) and the cover onto the tank. The film is now safely loaded in a lighttight tank, so you may take it out of your dark place—the rest of the developing process is done within the tank and thus can be done in daylight.

Developing Film

Check the instructions that came with your developer (more on photochemicals later), and bring the developer and the fixer (another chemical) to the recommended temperature. To do this, put the containers holding your developer and fixer into a deep pan of water that is adjusted to the recommended temperature. Yes, this does mean that you will have to buy a thermometer.

Measure the amount of developer needed and rapidly pour it through the top of the developing tank. Start timing development the moment you begin to pour in the developer (the developer's instructions will tell you how long you should develop your particular film). Once all the developer is in the tank, rap the tank bottom once or twice on the work surface. This will dislodge any air bubbles that may have stuck to the film. Now gently agitate the tank in the manner suggested in the tank's instructions. Do this every minute for ten seconds. When the developing time is completed, rapidly pour out the developer, saving it if it is a reusable type. In order to stop development, pour water into the tank, agitate, and pour out again. Repeat this step two more times, but be sure that the water temperature is within one or two degrees of the chemical's temperature. Failure to do so may ruin your negatives.

Fixing Baths

Now you must fix the film. Pour the required amount of fixer into the tank. Rap the tank bottom on the work surface, as before, agitate occasionally, and pour out the fixer after five to ten minutes. Less than five minutes will not be enough time to fix the film and more than ten minutes may damage the film. Save the fixer—it is reusable.

Washing Film

In order to remove all the remaining chemicals, you must wash the film for at least 30 minutes. Therefore, you will need a plastic container big enough to hold your film reel. Punch enough small holes in the bottom so that water will steadily and moderately run out. Next, put the developed film, still on its reel, into the plastic container, and put the container under the water tap. Rapidly fill the container with water at about the same temperature as your chemicals, then adjust the tap so that the water level will remain just above the top edge of the film.

Drying Film

When washing is complete, bathe the film in a wetting agent (Kodak Photo-Flo, for example). This will help you dry the film without water spots. Mix Photo-Flo exactly as directed. Too weak a solution will not work, and too strong a solution will streak the film. Take the film off the reel (you will probably be amazed now to see images on the film), and attach a spring-type clothes pin or a film clip to each end. Hang up the film in a dust-free, low-traffic, room-temperature place. Take a fresh piece of paper towel, folded to 3" x 5", and wipe down each side of the film once, very lightly, with the towel. It will normally take several hours for the film to dry thoroughly. If you need dry negatives in a hurry, Yankee Instant Film Dryer chemical can do the job in just a few minutes. Once dry, carefully cut the film into strips, six frames each (handle just the edge of the film), and insert the strips into negative-type envelopes. These envelopes will protect the negatives from all sorts of

misfortune and can be purchased from any camera store. They are available in sizes ranging from one page, just large enough for one strip of film, to entire pages, large enough to hold six or seven strips of film. Pages of negative strips can be stored loose-leaf style, with notes concerning content or exposure marked directly over any frame of film with a felt-tip marker. (Do not use the indelible type—use a Flair pen, a Write Brothers pen, or a Bic Banana.)

PHOTOCHEMICALS

Several types of film developers exist. Using a "one shot" type, prepare just the amount of developer that you immediately need and throw it away after one use. "One shot" is best for photographers who will seldom have film to develop and can thus be assured that the developer will always be fresh and at full strength.

A second kind of film developer is the "replenishment" variety. This type is completely mixed at one time and then replenished to full strength with another chemical after each use. Replenishment developers are a good choice if you develop film often, and they will cost you proportionally less per use than other developers.

Another type of developer works in two steps, or baths. It is usually expensive, but its use is most simple. In most cases, both time and temperature factors are not particularly critical as with all other developers.

Fixers stabilize film after development is completed and stopped. They are reusable and can process either film or prints. For best results, though, keep some fixer aside just for film and some just for prints. Be sure to mark the date of mixing on your fixer bottle. Most photochemicals have limited shelf life.

At this point in your photographic education, it is time for you to visit a very reliable tropical fish store. Ask the salesperson if it is necessary to use distilled water in an aquarium in your town. If he says yes, then there are too many minerals and other elements in the tap water for it to be used for mixing photographic chemicals, and you should buy distilled water for this purpose. If the salesperson says that local tap water may be used in aquariums, then it should be adequate for photochemicals.

Once your developer and fixer are mixed, you will need a dark, airtight container for storing them. Don't buy special photochemical bottles—you will be wasting money. Perfectly adequate, 40-ounce tinted bottles come with your purchase of Sunsweet, S. S. Pierce, and some Mott's juices —all with large, twist-on caps. If you wish to save even more, you can easily find these bottles at glass recycling centers. Larger containers of the one-half gallon variety can be had for free from your friendly neighborhood pharmacist. Remember to rinse out all remains of cough medicine or other drugs before using one of these jugs for your photographic chemicals.

To avoid spillage, you should buy a funnel to use when returning chemicals to their storage bottles. A big funnel is your best choice so that you can pour large quantities of liquid into it at a time. The best buy in funnels can be found at any discount, auto-parts store for about one-third of camera store prices for comparable merchandise.

It would be wise for you to filter each chemical after using it. If you buy paper filters, throw each away after pouring any one chemical through it. If you use a fine, mesh screen filter, wash it thoroughly after any filtration. For that matter, wash all your developing gear after each use. Never get any fixer in your developer; their properties negate one another. A very cheap filter medium is ordinary cotton. Just place a small ball in the neck of your funnel, and pour the chemical through the cotton wad.

COLOR FILM

You have no doubt noticed that there have been no instructions on color film or slide development. Due to the high cost and extreme difficulty of doing color darkroom work, it is definitely not recommended that you try it yet. If you feel you must dabble in color, Unicolor makes a kit for color slides called Unichrome, and it is fairly easy to use. Try this kit first. If you do not feel like going through all the work and expense of color processing, you can still send your film to a developing firm. Most photographers, amateur and professional alike, choose this route.

As you gaze proudly at your newly developed film, you may wonder how to change it into prints. Read on.

Take a good look at your home-developed negatives. You have probably noticed that their $1'' \times 1\frac{1}{2}''$ image size is conspicuously smaller than practically any photo you have ever seen. Therefore, you must enlarge the image size while making a photographic print.

Unfortunately, the minimal dark place that you used to load film into your developing tank will not be suitable for enlarging. Ideally, you should have a permanent darkroom with running water, but temporary quarters without a sink will suffice. Most people darken a bathroom or bedroom for this purpose. They do it by fitting heavy curtains or cardboard cut to size over the windows, in conjunction with towels to fill light leaks around the door. If these darkening attempts aren't sufficient, you will have to wait till sundown.

Your darkroom will have to be large enough to hold the following work surfaces: a table, supported board, or what have you, big enough to hold at least three $11'' \times 14''$ trays (room for four trays would be better); and a table or suitable substitute,

big enough to hold your enlarger. There should be a walkway in front of the work surfaces. Both surfaces must be sturdy and vibration free. If you choose to darken a bathroom, a wide board over the bathtub and another over the sink should provide you with enough room (Figure 7-1).

Your darkroom should be separated into two areas: a "dry" area that will hold your enlarger, photographic paper, and negatives; and a "wet" area on which you will put your trays of chemicals. These trays need not be the special, and usually overpriced, ones sold in camera stores. An inexpensive alternate is the average, plastic, kitty litter tray. Its sides are much higher than photo-processing trays and will prevent much spilling and slopping of chemicals. For your best buy, price them at large discount stores. You will also need two print tongs to handle the prints during the developing and fixing processes. Tongs with rubber tips are best so that you will not damage your prints. You need two so that one can be used only in the fixer and the other only in the developer and stop bath.

Figure 7-1

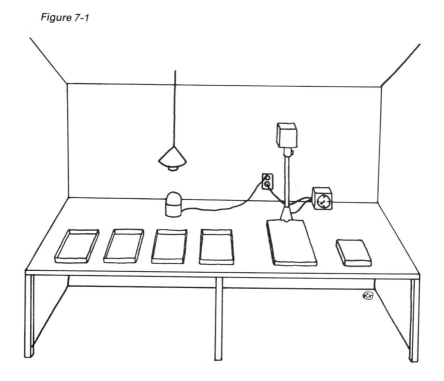

ENLARGING CHEMICALS

Enlarging requires the use of three or four chemicals: (1) paper developer; (2) 28% acetic acid stop bath or short stop; (3) fixer; and (4) a washing aid or hypo neutralizer, which is optional but recommended.

Paper developers "develop" the image on photographic paper in much the same manner that film developers do on film. They are sold as a liquid concentrate or as a powder that is mixed with water to become a liquid concentrate. The mixture is called a "stock solution." When you are ready to use the developer, dilute a portion of the stock solution according to manufacturer's instructions. Normally, you will be able to use the diluted chemical for only one session of printing. Some of the good paper developers that are readily available are Acufine Printofine, Agfa-Gevaert Metinol U, Kodak Dektol, and Ethol LPD—my favorite.

Once a print is sufficiently developed, you must stop the developing process before it causes the print to become too dark. This is best accomplished with a stop bath of 28% acetic acid, diluted according to its manufacturer's instructions. The stop bath that I suggested for use during film development is water, but you may use acetic acid solution if you prefer.

The fixer will stabilize the print and clear away any remaining undeveloped chemicals in the paper. All traces of the fixer must be removed after processing, or the print will eventually fade and turn brown. Therefore, prints have to be washed thoroughly. The fourth chemical, hypo neutralizer (also called a washing aid), will neutralize the remaining fixer and thus, reduce the time that your prints will have to be washed. Hypo neutralizer is not a required chemical, but it will save time and water.

PRINTING PAPERS

Many different photographic printing papers exist and may have any one of several surfaces, textures, tones, speeds, or contrast grades. Surfaces can range from mirror-like glossy to completely nonreflective matte. Glossy tends to show fine detail better than matte and is usually capable of rendering blacker tones. However, matte surfaces are fairly simple to "touch-up" with a No. 2 lead pencil and are free from distracting glare that often is reflected off glossy paper. Textures of paper also vary. You can buy anything from very smooth and lightly pebbled-surfaced paper to paper that looks and feels like linen or painter's canvas.

Paper tones range from a very cold-looking, almost blue tint through neutral whites and blacks to a warm, brownish appearance. In order to decide what tone and surface is best for your particular taste and needs, ask the camera salesmen at several stores to show you books of sample prints on different papers. Kodak, Luminos, Agfa-Gevaert, and Supreme, among others, supply their dealers with such sample books.

Paper speeds are rather inexact and are often referred to as slow, moderate, fast, and very fast. For most normal enlarging, fast paper is the most convenient choice. It is fast enough to keep you from going to sleep during exposure, but slow enough to allow you to do some advanced darkroom tricks. Slow paper is usually designed for contact prints (more on these later).

Photographic paper is sold in several contrast grades. Papers that will produce very low-contrast prints are graded "0" and "1." Grade number "2" is considered normal contrast, and grades "3" and "4" are hard or high contrast. (Agfa-Gevaert paper is available in super high-contrast grades "5" and "6.") These grades are made so that you may compensate for contrast variations in your negatives and also produce special effects. For maximum versatility, you should keep several paper grades on hand. Or you can stock just one paper if it is a variable-contrast type. Variable-contrast (VC) papers require that you also buy special filters that make the paper respond as though it were any one of several contrast grades. Filters for one brand of VC paper may not work properly with other brands. Two of the most easily found VC papers are Kodak Polycontrast and DuPont Varilour.

ENLARGING EASELS

You will need an enlarging easel to hold the printing paper flat and to help you "crop" your photos. The most common variety of easel consists of a flat baseboard and a hinged frame that lays on top of it. One corner and its two adjacent sides are fixed to one another and the other two sides can slide both in and out. This allows you to crop the photo, visually cutting off certain sections of the picture by sliding the movable sides until the desired portion of

the image lies within the easel's four sides (Figure 7-2).

If you neglected to apply the rule of thirds when taking your photos (see Chap. 3), you can make use of it now. Referring back to Figure 3-3, shift the easel's position around until the subject is at a spot corresponding to one of the points of intersection, or until the horizon lies one-third of the way in from the top or bottom of the picture area.

Adjustable easels are the most versatile, and in all probability, will be your best choice to buy. Be sure to choose one that is large enough to handle most of your enlarging needs—usually 8″ x 10″.

If you do buy an adjustable 8″ x 10″ easel and occasionally plan to make larger prints (11″ x 14″ or 16″ x 20″), you can invert a dime-store, metal picture frame and slide your paper in and out as shown in Figure 7-3. Save the glass. It will come in handy when you want to make contact prints.

SAFELIGHTS

Total darkness is not necessary when you are printing black-and-white photos. You will need a "safelight." A safelight is a low-

Figure 7-2

intensity, colored light that will not affect printing paper. An amber colored safelight is fine for use with most papers, but in some cases, a different color light is required. Check the paper manufacturer's instructions concerning safelights before exposing the paper to any light. *Never* open a box of printing paper except under suggested safelight conditions. *Always* keep boxes of paper closed except for the brief moment it takes you to remove a needed sheet.

If space and money allow, you should have two safelights: one near the fixer tray and the other near the enlarger. You can make do with just one, though, if your "wet" and "dry" areas are fairly close together. The cost of safelights can range from $6 to $80 for units that are screwed into standard sockets, are mounted on walls, are hung from the ceiling, or are free standing. Some very reasonable ($6 to $8), free-standing units that would suffice are made by Paterson and Ilford. You will also need a white light near the fixer tray that you can switch on and off to inspect your prints after fixing them. Incidentally, this book is not an advertisement for Paterson products. I just happen to like their well-designed product line.

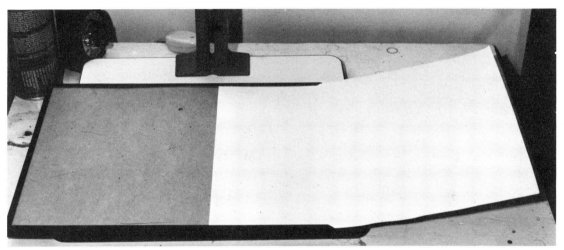

Figure 7-3

ENLARGERS

The central, and most expensive, object in your darkroom will be your enlarger. There are many enlargers on the market, costing anywhere from $35 to over $1,000. All of them enlarge the negative by projecting its image onto a flat surface.

The format size of an enlarger should be your first consideration. Often, people who began photography using the 35mm format discover that they want to work with cameras that use larger film, such as 2¼" x 2¼" (120 or 220 size film) or 4" x 5". Thus, if they initially bought an enlarger that was unable to operate with anything larger than 35mm film, they would have to purchase a bigger enlarger along with their bigger camera. Therefore, even though you may save money on your first enlarger purchase, you may eventually have to buy one or two more enlargers, if you decide to use a bigger format camera. Since any well-built enlarger will last at least 20 years, carefully consider making it a one-time expenditure.

Once you decide what format enlarger to buy, inspect the models available for solidity of construction, freedom from shake, quality of materials, ease of cleaning, and method of holding negatives. A solidly built enlarger made from good materials will last a long time. It must be wobble-free, if you are to expect good results. If the enlarger shakes or flexes while in use, your prints will be blurred.

Just as dust was your foe while shooting and developing film, it is an even more formidable enemy when you are making enlargements. Any dust adhering to the negative or glass surfaces of your enlarger will be enlarged along with the images on the negative. Therefore, while trying to decide upon an enlarger, check all the possible candidates for ease of cleaning. You can save many hours of work if your enlarger is easy to clean.

If you plan to do mostly black-and-white printing, which is most likely, make sure that the enlarger you buy uses a condenser-illumination system. This design will produce sharper, more contrasty prints than a diffusion-illuminated enlarger. Diffusion illumination, though, is the better choice for color printing.

Determine if the enlarger you select is capable of holding negatives good and flat. If it accomplishes this feat by holding the negative on, against, or between glass, be sure that the glass is treated to prevent "Newton's rings." Newton's rings are a phenomenon that causes transitory wood-grain-like rings to appear between the glass and the negative, and these are projected onto the print.

Enlarger Lenses

If a lens is not sold with your enlarger, you will need one to focus the negative's images onto photoprinting paper. The most deluxe enlarging lenses are made by Leitz, Nikon, and Schneider. However, almost any enlarging lens will operate more than adequately if its aperture is closed down about two f/stops from maximum before exposure. You will need a lens with a focal length of 50mm for 35mm film enlargement and 75mm for $2^1/_4'' \times 2^1/_4''$ film.

As a final consideration, you should investigate how large a print an enlarger can make on its baseboard, and how easily it can swing or swivel to a position that will allow it to produce even bigger prints. A serious limitation on the size of enlargement will prove frustrating enough to cause you to scrap a brand new enlarger.

Some of my favorite enlargers on the market are listed below. Many other good ones exist.

Manufacturer	Model No.	Maximum film size	Remarks
Beseler	23C	$2^1/_4'' \times 3^1/_4''$	Exceedingly sturdy. Condenser adjusts for other films.
Beseler	45M	$4'' \times 5''$	
Durst	M700	$2^1/_4'' \times 3^1/_4''$	Extremely rugged. Calibrated support. Easy to clean.
Durst	M601	$2^1/_4'' \times 2^1/_4''$	
Durst	M301	35mm	Compact. Easy to clean.
Paterson	35	35mm	Built-in easel.
Simmon Omega	D2C	$4'' \times 5''$	Very sturdy. Changeable condensers.
Simmon Omega	B-22	$2^1/_4'' \times 2^1/_4''$	

TIMERS

Time control is very important when making photographic prints. For this reason, you will need some sort of timer. The least expensive alternative is to use a sweep secondhand, radium-dial alarm clock to time development and fixing and to count off seconds (1,001, 1,002, etc.) during the actual exposure of the photographic paper. Though this is cheap, it is not the preferred method.

The first runner-up to the least expensive choice (and a somewhat better choice, at that) is the 0 to 60 second spring-wound timer for use during exposure. They are sold from about $6 and can turn an enlarger on and off for any increment of time that you set on it. Use the radium-dial alarm clock to time development and fixing. Far more expensive timers exist, but the combination of the two clocks above will prove adequate.

If you can justify the expenditure, a costly darkroom timer is very nice to have. This class of equipment often has such features as automatic resetting to a preselected time, foot-actuating switch, and an audible signal every second (we'll see the potential of this feature in a moment, when we discuss test strips).

PRINTING

Assuming that you now have all the enlarging equipment you need, your chemicals are mixed, and your darkroom is dark, you are ready to begin printing.

Set out your trays and chemicals as shown in Figure 7-1. Put about one inch of developer and water solution into the left-hand tray, one inch of diluted stop bath into the second tray, and about two inches of fixer into the third tray. If you have a fourth tray, put at least two inches of water into it. Switch on your safelight(s), and switch off normal room lights.

Contact Prints

It is very difficult to determine from a negative whether it will turn out to be a good picture. For this reason, it is suggested that you make contact prints of all your negatives. A contact print is so called because it is made by putting a negative in direct contact with paper and then exposing and processing the paper (Figure 7-4).

Adjust your enlarger so that its light will more than cover an 8″ x 10″ area on its baseboard, and switch off its light. Take a portion of glossy printing paper (perhaps 2″ x 2″ and place it, emulsion side up, in the middle of the area that will be lighted by your enlarger. You can tell the emulsion side of paper in one of two ways: (1) paper will often curl toward its emulsion side; and (2) paper is usually shinier on its emulsion side. Now place a negative strip on top of the paper, emulsion side down, and cover with a piece of clean glass. Negative emulsion is on the less shiny surface of the film, and the negative also tends to curl toward the emulsion side.

Stop down your enlarger lens to f/11, and

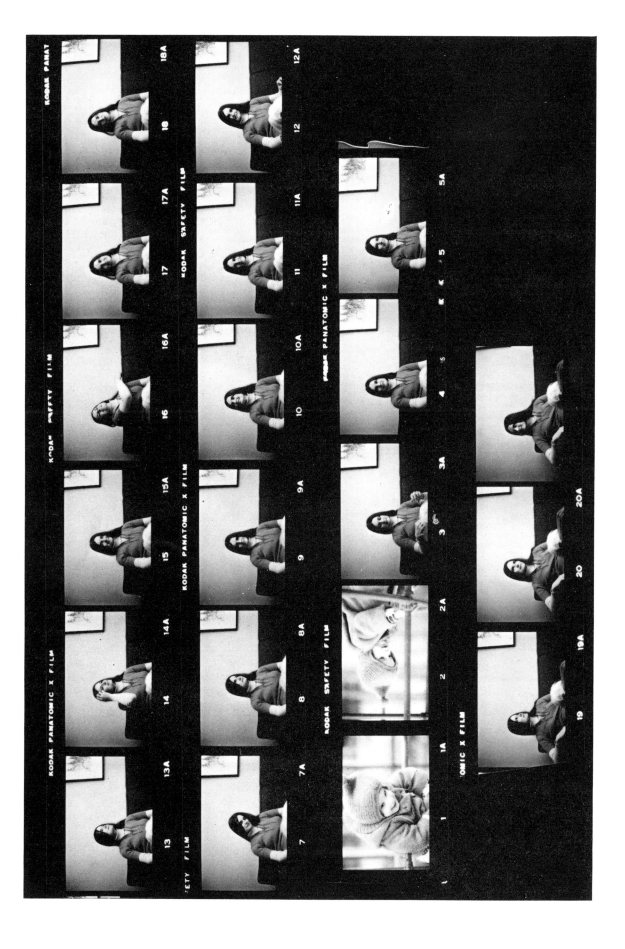

expose the paper for 3 seconds if you are using regular enlarging paper or 30 seconds if you are using contact printing paper. Immerse the paper, face up, into the developer and gently agitate the tray for the amount of time suggested in your developer's instructions (usually one-and-one-half to two minutes). Take the paper out of the developer ten seconds before the development time has expired and let it drain off into the tray. At the end of the 10 seconds, immerse the paper in the stop bath for 30 seconds. Hold it over the stop bath to drain off, then put the paper into the fixer. Occasionally agitate the tray. After two minutes of fixing, you can inspect the print in white light to see if it is properly exposed. If the highlights are not washed out and the shadow areas are not too black, obscuring details, the print has been properly exposed. If it is too light, you will have to try again, turning on your enlarger for a longer time. If the print is far too light, start by doubling the exposure time. If it is too dark, you will have to make another, shorter exposure.

Once you have zeroed in on a good exposure time, put an entire 8″ x 10″ sheet of paper, emulsion side up, on the enlarger's baseboard. Then, place as many strips of negative as will fit side by side on the paper, emulsion side down. The absolute maximum number that will fit is six strips of six frames each. Cover the negatives and paper with a sheet of clean glass, expose, and then process. This time, though, let the print remain in the fixer for the full amount of time recommended by its manufacturer (usually five to ten minutes). When fixing is complete, put the print into a tray of water.

Instead of using a plain piece of glass to hold the negatives and paper flat, you may buy a contact-proof printer, designed to hold 35mm film. This would make contact printing easier, but it is not an absolute necessity.

By viewing your contact prints with a critical eye, you will be able to decide which negatives are worth your effort to enlarge.

No matter how carefully you have handled your negatives, they have probably picked up some dust that will have to be removed before enlarging. Using a can of compressed, moisture-free air (marketed under the names of "Omit" and "Dust Off"), blow off any dust adhering to the negative below the enlarging lens with the enlarger's lamp switched on. Dust will be most visible in such light. If there is any glass surface in your enlarger within a half-inch of the negative carrier, blow it clean, also.

Printing Negatives

Insert the selected negative into your enlarger's negative carrier, emulsion side down, with the image upside down (the enlarger will project it right side up, thus making it easier for you to perceive the picture once it is projected onto the baseboard). Take one sheet of printing paper out of its box and place it in your enlarging easel. Switch on your enlarger, adjust its height so that the image is the size you want it to be, and carefully focus the image on the paper that you put in the easel. Always focus on a sheet of paper that is as thick as the paper you plan to expose. Even the difference between having paper in the easel or not can change the focus of the image. Focus your enlarger with its lens at maximum aperture. The more light that is available, the easier it will be to focus.

Figure 7-4

Grain-Focusing Devices

A more accurate method of focusing involves the use of grain-focusing devices. A grain-focusing device costs anywhere from $4 to nearly $100, with most models priced below $15. It magnifies a portion of an image that is projected by the enlarger so that you can focus on the actual clumps of grain rather than the overall picture. To use one, first adjust your enlarger so that a negative is projected onto your easel at the same size as the final print you want. Place a sheet of photoprinting paper in the easel, coarse focus the enlarger by eye, and place the grain-focusing device on the paper in the middle of the easel. Stop down the enlarging lens to the f/stop you will probably use for the final print. This will make for more accurate focusing when using a grain-focusing device and will be easier on your eyes. Peer through the eyepiece of the grain-focusing device, and adjust the enlarger's focus control until you see the sharpest, clearest image of grain.

If you decide to buy a grain-focusing device, see if you can purchase it on a trial basis, because one that works well for some people may not work well for you.

Once focused, stop down the lens two or three stops, unless you focused at printing aperture with a grain-focusing device. Switch off the enlarger and remove the focusing sheet of paper. Put it aside for later use.

Test Strips

Take a fresh sheet of 8″ x 10″ enlarging paper out of its box and cut it into five 2″ x 8″ pieces. Place one strip of paper, emulsion side up, in the middle of the easel (or in the most important section of the print), and return the rest to their box. Cover the strip on the easel with your focusing sheet of paper. Put the sweep secondhand clock or timer right next to the easel (or have a companion call off seconds to you or use an audible, signaling timer) and switch on the enlarger. Uncover approximately a ¼″ x 8″ section of the test strip. After two seconds, expose another quarter-inch section of the test strip. At this point, a half-inch section should be exposed. Wait two more seconds and expose another quarter-inch section. Do this until all eight quarter-inch sections of the test strip have been exposed. Switch off the enlarger and process your test strip through the developer, stop bath, and fixer.

Switch on the inspection light and you will notice that the test strip is composed of eight quarter-inch strips that are progressively darker due to their two-second increases of exposure. If any of these strips, other than the 2-second or 16-second ones, looks best, use the exposure time of that strip for your final print (Figure 7-5). If the two-second exposure looks best, stop down the lens one more stop and run a new test strip. If the 16-second strip looks best, run another test strip, but give the entire piece of paper an extra 10 seconds of exposure. Then, inspect the new strip for a well-exposed portion and use its exposure time for the final print. The reason why you should not accept the shortest or longest exposed portions of your test strip is that an even better exposure may exist beyond these bounds.

Figure 7-5

WASHING PRINTS

Having determined the proper exposure for your final print, expose and process the picture as you did with the contact sheets. When you are through enlarging, you will have to wash all of your prints thoroughly. If, in your great wisdom, you bought a washing aid or hypo neutralizer, soak and agitate your prints in it for as long as the instructions tell you. To be sure that all the chemicals are removed, wash the prints for 10% longer than the washing aid's manufacturer tells you, in water that is about 80 degrees Fahrenheit. If you didn't use a washing aid, wash your prints for at least one hour.

There are many devices sold to help you wash your prints. If you don't want to spend anything on a print washer, though, you may fill a sink or tub with water, immerse your prints in it, and agitate. However, every five minutes for one hour, you will have to drain the water, refill, and agitate again.

Testrite and De Hypo make inexpensive print washers in the $5 to $6 range that resemble print trays. They drain themselves continuously, thus saving you the effort. A low-cost alternate is Kodak tray siphon, designed for print washing. It adds fresh water to a print tray while drawing off chemical-laden water from the bottom.

Two very good units are manufactured by Testrite and Paterson. The Testrite washers are drum-shaped and cause the incoming water to swirl around the prints, efficiently removing hypo. More expensive, but very conservative in their use of water, are the Paterson print washers. They provide constant automatic agitation for your prints, insuring excellent wash characteristics.

I have known people who have built their own print washers out of baby bathinettes or round washtubs. If you design one yourself, remember to draw off the heavier, chemical-laden water from the bottom and provide agitation.

DRYING PRINTS

Once your prints are washed, they must be dried. The simplest method is to hang plastic screening or cheesecloth horizontally across a room. The prints are squeegeed and placed, face down, on the mesh until dry. To squeegee your prints, place them against a flat, vertical surface, such as a refrigerator door. Then, remove most of the water by rolling a print roller over the print or by wiping it with a squeegee. A drawback of the mesh-drying method is that your prints will curl up quite a bit (if you use double-weight paper, this problem will be reduced).

A more satisfactory way to dry your prints is between photographic "blotter" pages that are chemically neutral. After squeegeeing off any surface water, put each photo between a pair of blotters and stack them up for about 15 minutes. Then, put each print between two pairs of dry blotters, stack all the blotter-print groupings into one pile, and weigh it down with some large books. In a few hours, your prints will be dry and flat.

Electric Print Dryers

You may buy an electric print dryer if you prefer, but for best results, be sure to use it only at its lower temperature settings. High-er settings will often damage the prints. If your electric dryer has a chrome surface, it can be used to "ferrotype" your print (make a glossy-surfaced paper super shiny). To do this, thoroughly clean the metal plate with water, but don't dry it off. Place a squeegeed print, face down, on the plate, and turn the dryer control on to a low setting. Let the print dry for at least ten minutes. For nonglossy-surfaced papers, dry them face up.

If you want ferrotyped prints but don't have a ferrotyping print dryer, don't want to go through the required work, or just can't get the hang of it, you can buy a special paper made by Luminos or Kodak. It dries to a very high sheen after a short time.

Luminos Rapid Dry and Kodak Polycontrast Rapid RC are resin-coated to prevent the paper from becoming soaked with chemicals. Hence, either paper may be used without an acid stop bath (just water will do). Much abbreviated washing and drying times are two more resultant advantages—truly an accomplishment equal to the discovery of fire, the invention of the wheel, and the development of soft-serve ice cream.

DARKROOM TRICKS

No matter how carefully you have composed, exposed, developed, and printed your photos, there will be times when the final print won't seem quite right. Sometimes portions of a photo will print perfectly while other parts will be too dark or too light. The solution to this problem is in the form of some basic darkroom tricks called "dodging" and "burning-in."

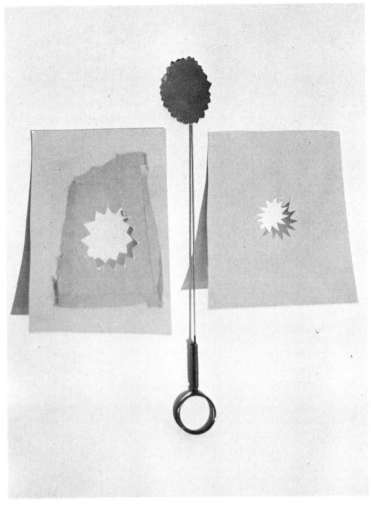

Dodging

Figure 7-6

Areas in a photo that are too dark have been given too much exposure to the enlarger's light. In order to keep those areas from becoming too dark, you must reduce their exposure. Do this by blocking the light for part of the exposure—a process referred to as dodging. The best tools to use for dodging are either your hands or a piece of cardboard, taped to a stiff wire (Figure 7-6).

Dodge as follows. After determining the overall, proper exposure, make a test strip of that portion that will print dark to determine its proper exposure. Then, expose the print normally for the amount of time need-ed to expose the dark areas. At the end of that time, put your dodging tool between the enlarger and the print so that it blocks anymore light from reaching the dark areas (these will appear light in the negative image). Continue exposing the rest of the print for as long as previously determined. One caution: If you leave your dodging tool motionless in the light path, there will be a distinct, unnatural border in your print surrounding the dodged area. To avoid this, you should move the dodging tool up and down throughout the dodging portion of the exposure, without any lateral movement.

Burning-In

Burning-in is dodging in reverse. In this instance, a section of a print that is too light must be given more exposure (be burned-in) so that it will appear dark enough in the final print. To determine how much exposure is necessary, you will have to make a test print. Following that, expose a sheet of paper for the amount of time needed for most of the print. At the end of that time, insert a burning-in tool (your hands or a piece of cardboard cut similar to the right-hand item in Figure 7-6) in the light path so that only the area needing more exposure is not blocked. Move your burning-in tool up and down in the same manner as your dodging tool. At the end of the additional exposure time, switch off the enlarger and develop the print.

Figure 7-7 is not a very good print. To make it better, the eaves must be dodged and the bright area to the right must be burned-in. Figure 7-8 has been dodged and burned-in as follows. Test strips told me that the overall print required an exposure of 14 seconds, the eaves required 9 seconds, and the bright area required 20 seconds. I exposed the entire paper for 9 seconds and then blocked the eaves for another 5 seconds (total 14 seconds). Then, I blocked all but the bright area for another 6 seconds, giving a total exposure of 20 seconds there. The results? Details are visible from the lightest to the darkest sections of the print. This entire process was continuous without switching off the enlarger until the end. Dodging and burning-in can save some poor exposures, but don't bank on them. Expose the film properly for consistently good results.

Vignettes

Figure 7-9 was printed by utilizing a variation of dodging called a "vignette." For effect, I decided to print this picture without any detail surrounding the subject. To do this, I blocked the area surrounding the baby's face with the burning-in tool pictured in Figure 7-6, on the right. Had I wanted to vignette a photo of an older woman instead, I would have used the dodging–burning-in tool pictured on the left of Figure 7-6. This tool is virtually the same as the tool on the right except that it has a piece of stocking taped over its opening. The stocking will slightly diffuse light passing through it, thus softening shadows and wrinkles. The stocking will also prevent some light from reaching the print, thus requiring a longer exposure time. Therefore, the test print must be made with the stocking in place between the enlarger and the paper.

COLOR PRINTING

Color printing and enlarging are frighteningly difficult and expensive. The required chemicals have a very short life and must be discarded fairly soon after mixing. To produce acceptable prints, you must use numerous filters and buy some costly accessories. If you feel you should try color printing, though, there is a relatively easy-to-use, moderate-cost kit made by Aeroprint. When used with slides instead of color negatives and the appropriate printing paper, you can make "straight" prints that don't require color-printing filters. As a bonus, the Aeroprint color chemicals will last up to two years before spoiling. Unfortunately, it is a very time-consuming and messy process. The process is somewhat simplified (when printing from slides) if you substitute an ordinary paper developer such as Dektol for the first Aeroprint developer mentioned in their slide-printing instructions.

Figure 7-7

Figure 7-8

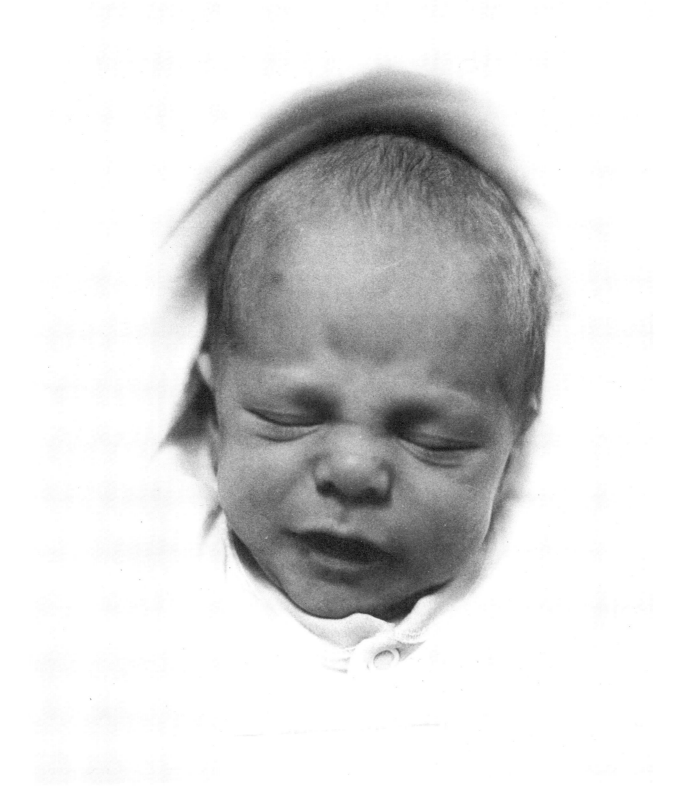

Figure 7-9

8
ALMOST THE END

If you have come this far and have successfully performed all of the photo-magic feats I have described, you are no doubt excited and possibly somewhat frustrated. Where can you go from here?

First, look up any friends of yours who happen to be professional photographers or who are very good amateurs. If they are really friends rather than acquaintances, they will be glad to critique your photos both for content and technical quality. Ask for their advice every time you make new photos that seem good to you.

Second, invest in any of the following highly recommended publications.

Petersen's PhotoGraphic Magazine. A monthly magazine that is filled with thoroughly explained instructive articles on various techniques and gadgetry. This is a "must buy" publication once you become an intermediate or advanced photographer.

Leica Manual and Data Book. Buy any edition, from the most recent to one 15 years old. Morgan & Morgan publishes this book, designed for all 35mm photography—not just Leica. It is loaded with data, physical principles, Leica equipment, and "how to do it" instructions.

Photo-Lab-Index. Also published by Morgan & Morgan, this Index is only for those of you who have just about become advanced photographers. It is an immense, loose-leaf book that contains nearly every technical detail concerning the taking and processing of pictures. It may be kept current through quarterly mailed updates.

Also investigate books and pamphlets published by Kodak, Amphoto, and Morgan & Morgan.

The balance of this book will concern five final handy hints (FHH).

FHH No. 1. It is likely that when you bought your camera a case came with it. Manufacturers call them "eveready cases," but most experienced photographers call them other names (the most polite one being "never-ready cases"). If one of these cases came with your camera, detach the front portion anytime that you take the camera out of its storage place. If you leave the front of the case on the camera when you embark on a photo trip or session, you will miss many good shots as you fumble with the case, or you will decide that it is too much trouble to open it up. Further, jostling or the wind may make the case cover the lens just at the moment you take the picture. You can, and should, leave the back-bottom portion of the case on your camera. Leaving the back-bottom portion on will help protect the camera and will prevent you from inadvertently pushing the rewind-release button. Also, always keep the lens cap on the lens anytime that you are not composing and shooting. It will protect your lens from mishap.

FHH No. 2. Batteries, film, and photographic printing paper are all perishable items. Their shelf life can be extended almost indefinitely if they are wrapped in plastic and stored in a refrigerator. However, you should allow these items to warm up to the ambient temperature before using. Paper should be at room temperature to react properly with chemicals. Film and batteries may form harmful condensation, if they are allowed to warm up in the camera or flash.

FHH No. 3. An extremely handy accessory for you to own is a "changing bag." It is a completely lighttight, black cloth bag with two elastic-rimmed holes for your hands to pass through. It can be used anywhere to load film into developing tanks or to check your camera mid-roll for film breakage or misalignment. If you plan to use infrared-sensitive film, a changing bag is a must. Except for actual picture-taking, infrared-film cartridges should never be exposed to light until they are developed. Therefore, you should load and unload your camera in the total darkness of a darkroom or a changing bag.

FHH No. 4. Constantly be on the alert for anything that appears unusual—strange and different lighting, humorous or out-of-place tableaus, and ordinary objects in extraordinary environments. Any such situation may prove to be the subject of an outstanding photograph. Figure 7-10 is just such a picture. Usually, photos of pets are boring to anyone who doesn't have an emotional attachment to such animals. However, Figure 8-1 works because of its

Figure 8-1

unusual treatment of an ordinary subject.

FHH No. 5. The least expensive object in the hobby of photography is film, especially black-and-white. Take advantage of this relative bargain by using a lot of film. Don't be afraid to shoot numerous extra photos, freely experimenting with the techniques mentioned in earlier chapters. This will allow you to sharpen your skills through practice. As a result, many of these pictures will be disappointing, but others will begin to show promise. Keep a log on what you have done (shutter speeds, *f*/stops, lenses,

films) so that you will begin to have a feel of what factors affect your successful photos.

If by now you are not completely hooked on photography, it is unlikely that you will ever be. If you are hooked, try to expand your capabilities through photography courses, much reading, and fearless experimentation. Photography is a boundless medium. So much of a successful photograph is in the eye and imagination of the photographer.

96